COLORING WILD AFRICA

By R.L. CLEBERT

All Rights Reserved. © Copyright R. L. CLEBERT 2017

Disclaimer

No part of this book may be reproduced or transmitted in any form or by any means, mechanical or electronic, including photocopying or recording, or by an information storage and retrieval system, or transmitted by e-mail without permission in writing from the publisher. This book is for entertainment purposes only. The views expressed are those of the author alone.

Published by

PANGEA ART Inc

Tampa, Fl 02062

www.PANGEAUNIVERSAL.com

@pangea_publishing

www.depositephotos.com

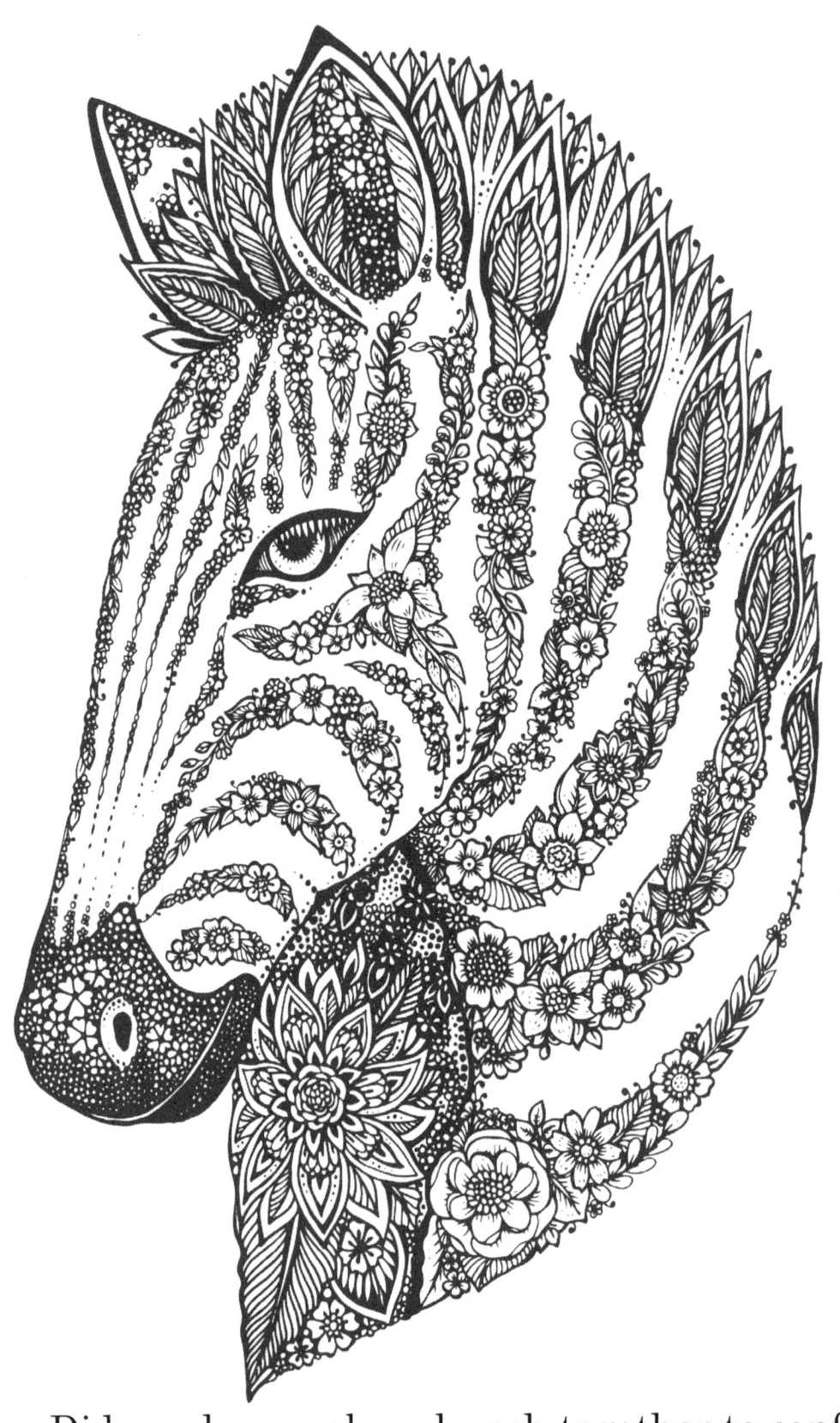

Did you know zebras bunch together to confuse colorblind predators such as Lions

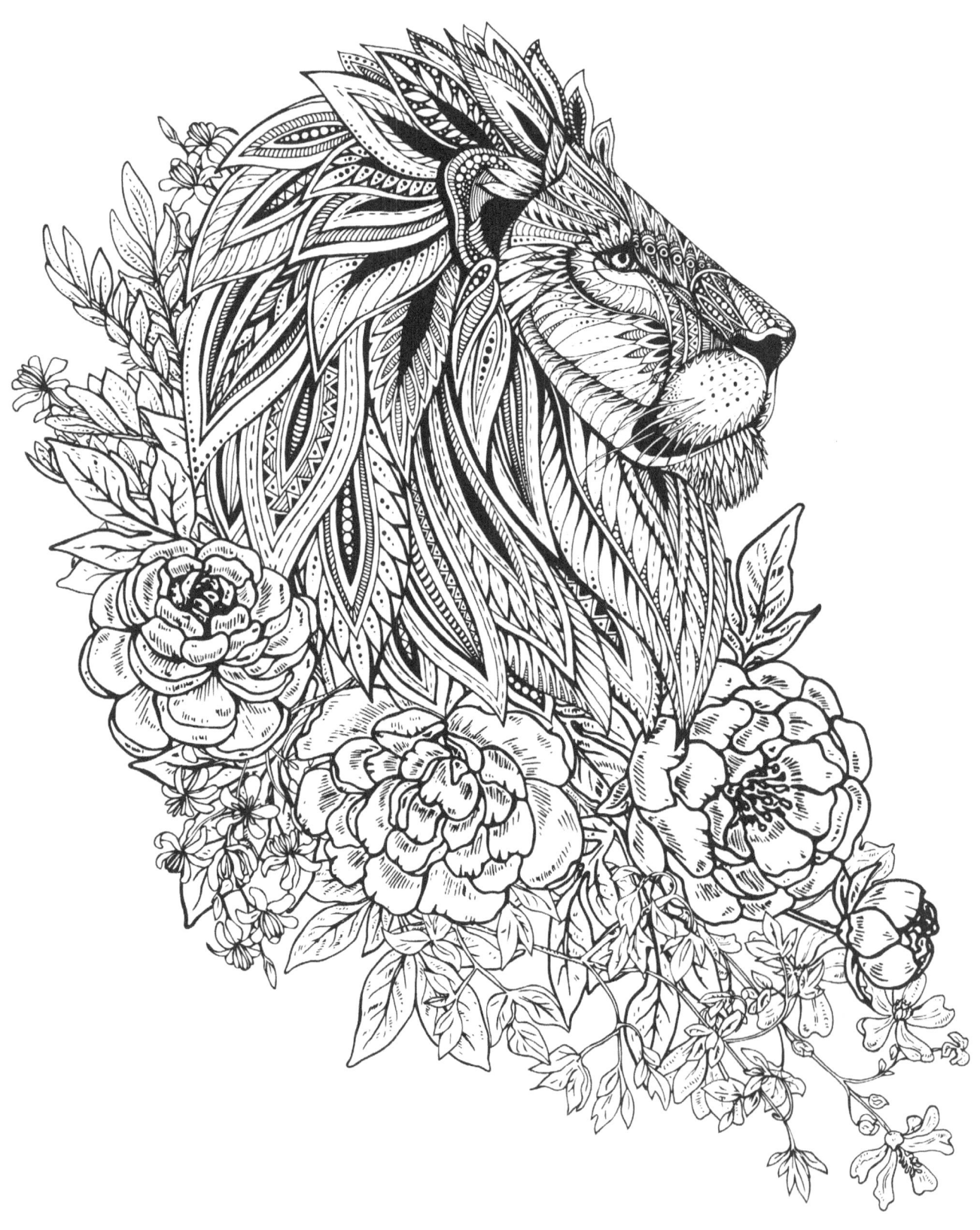

A lion's roar can be heard from as far as 5 miles away

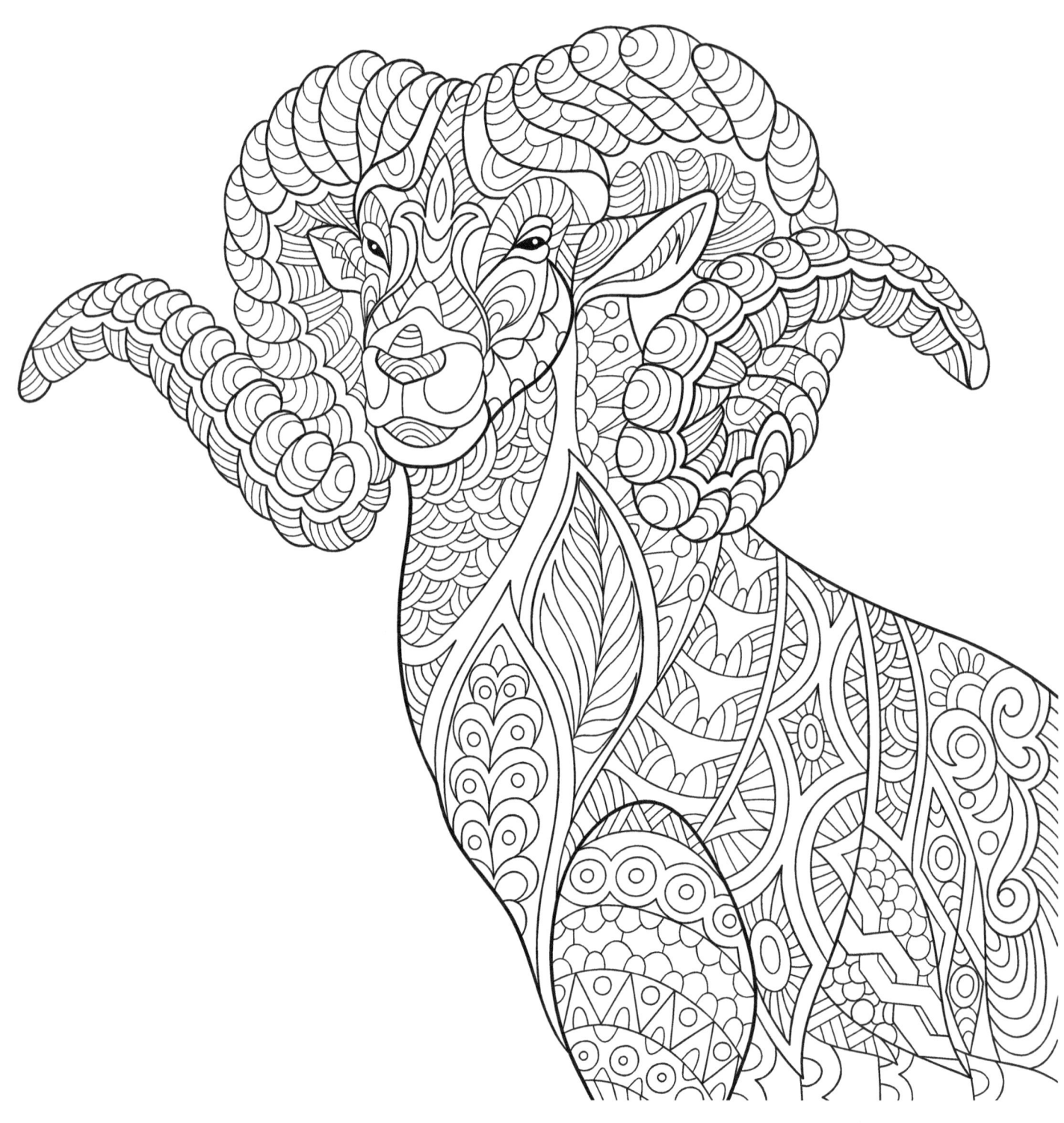

Horn Size Is A Symbol Of Rank. Male Horns Can Weigh As Much As 30 lbs

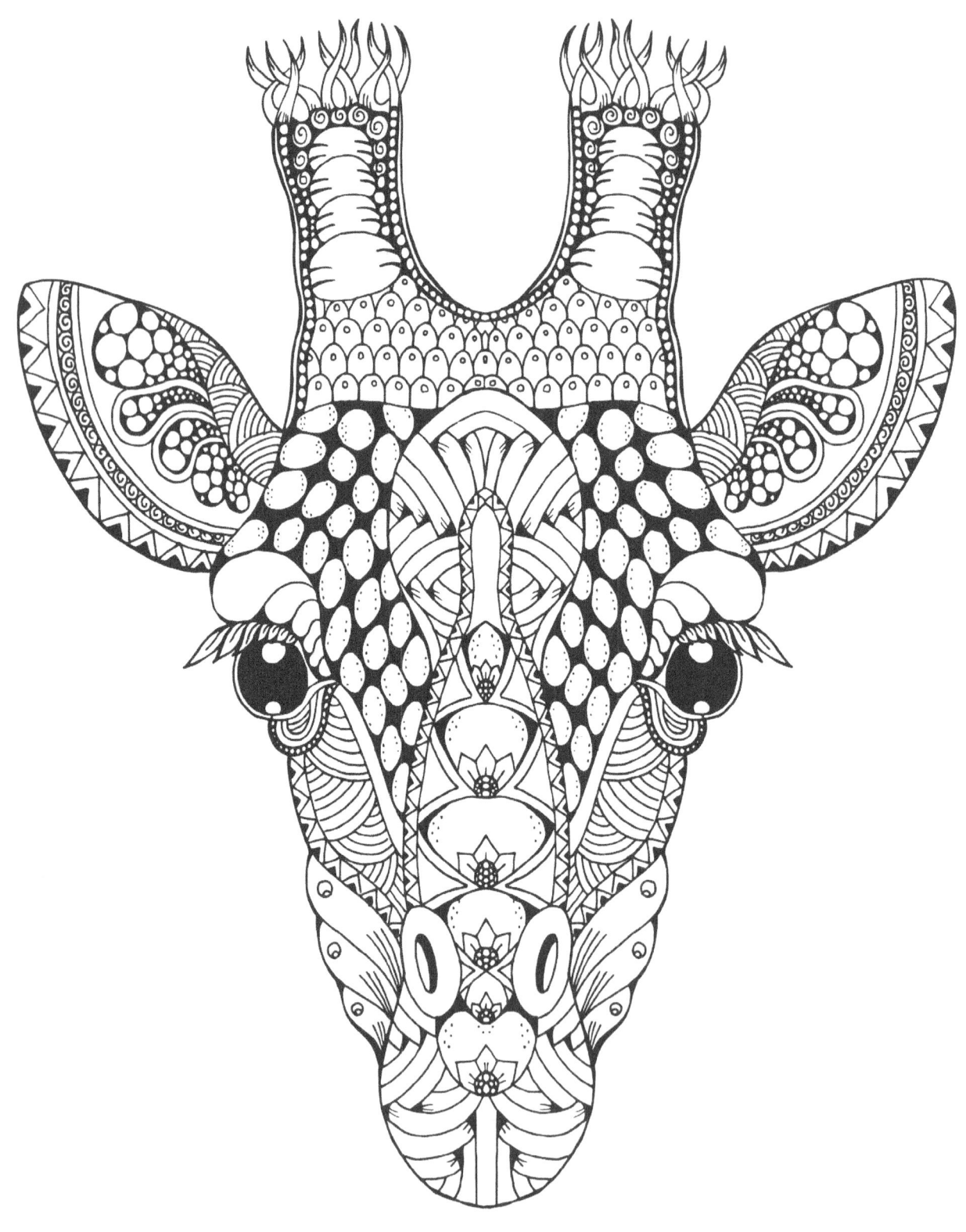

Giraffes Heart It's Two Feet Long And Weighs Up To 25 Pounds.

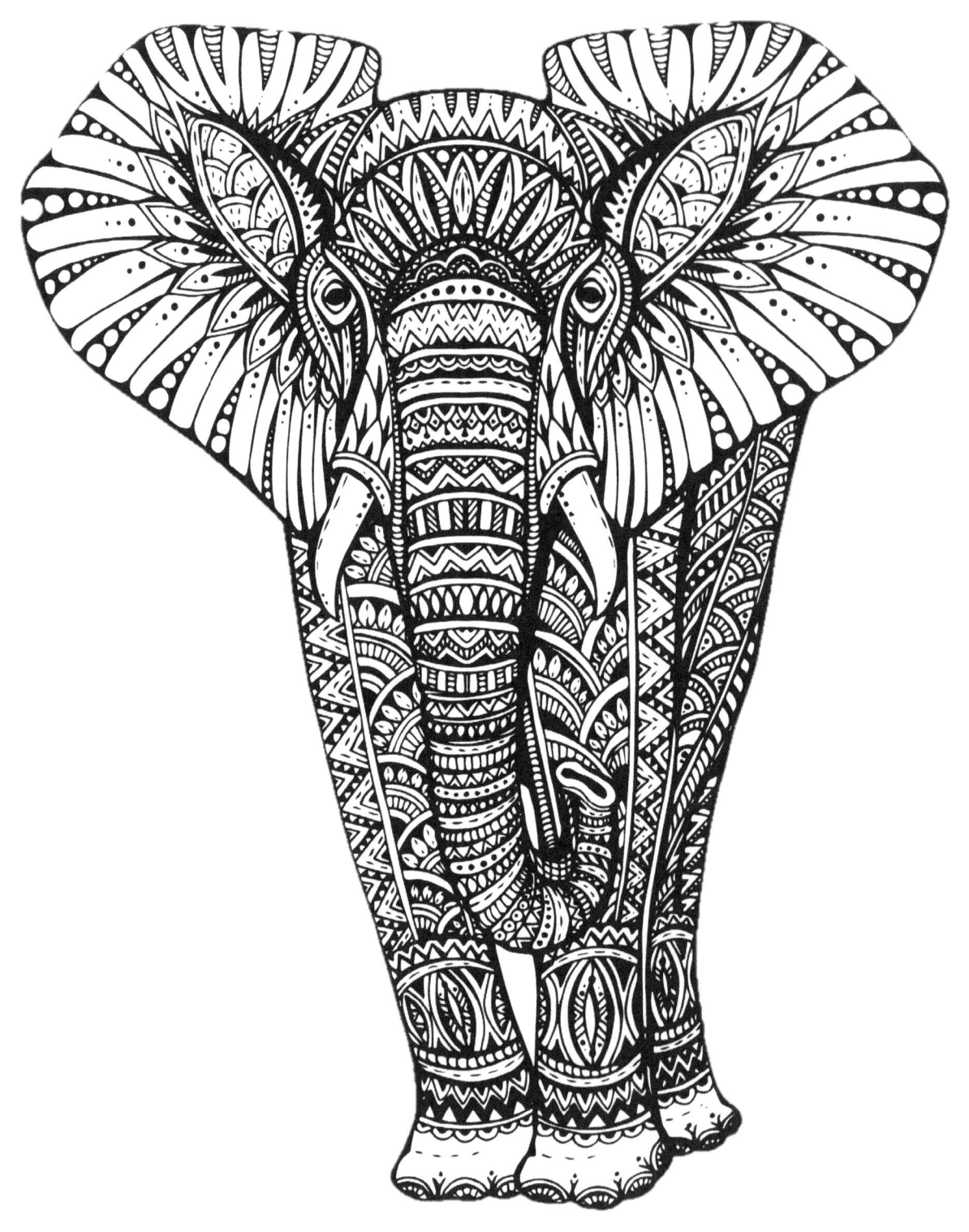

Elephant Females Undergo The Longest Gestation Period Of All Mammals - They Are Pregnant For 22 Months.

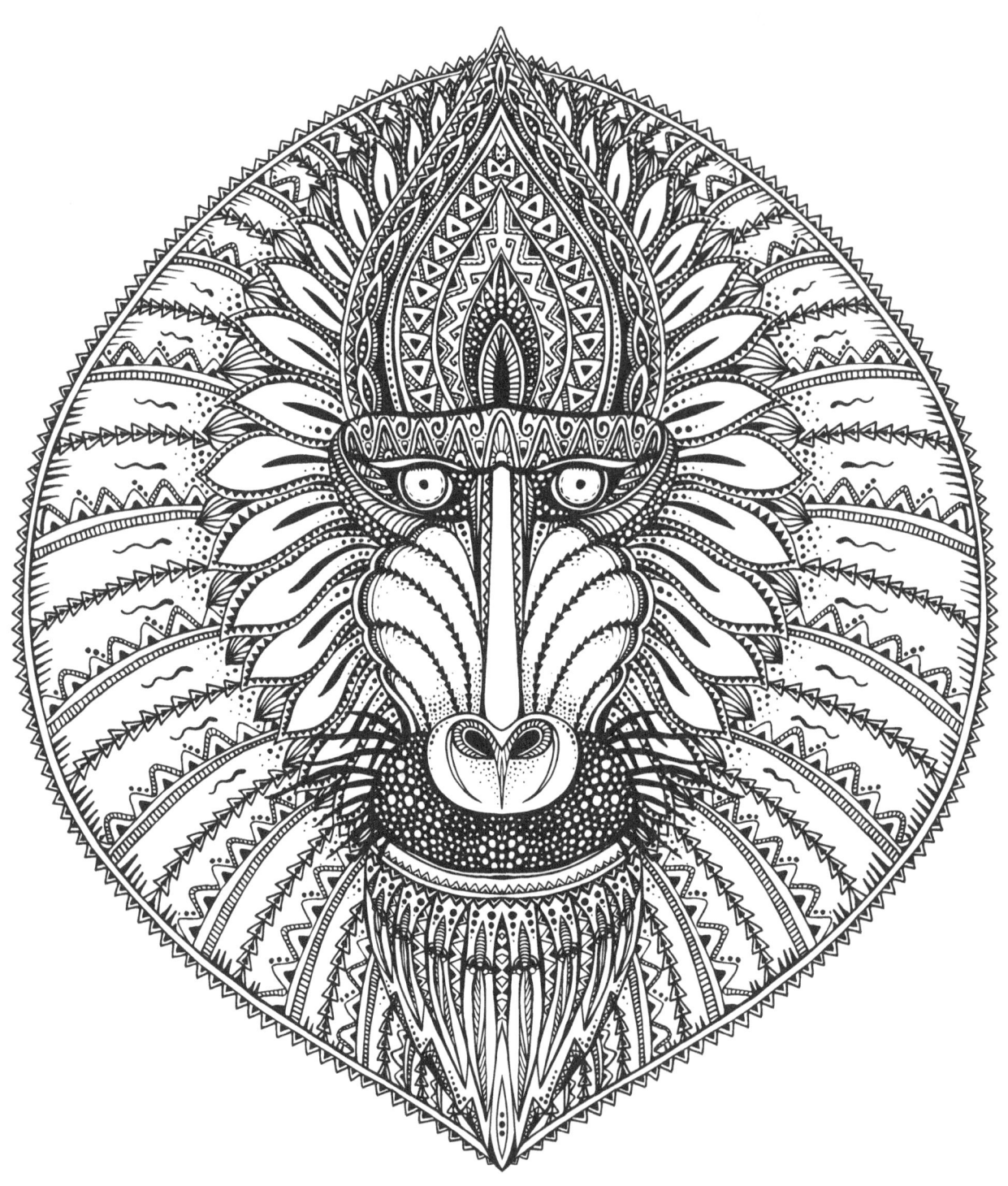

When A Female Baboon Is Ready To Mate, Her Bottom Becomes Swollen And Red As A Sign To The Males

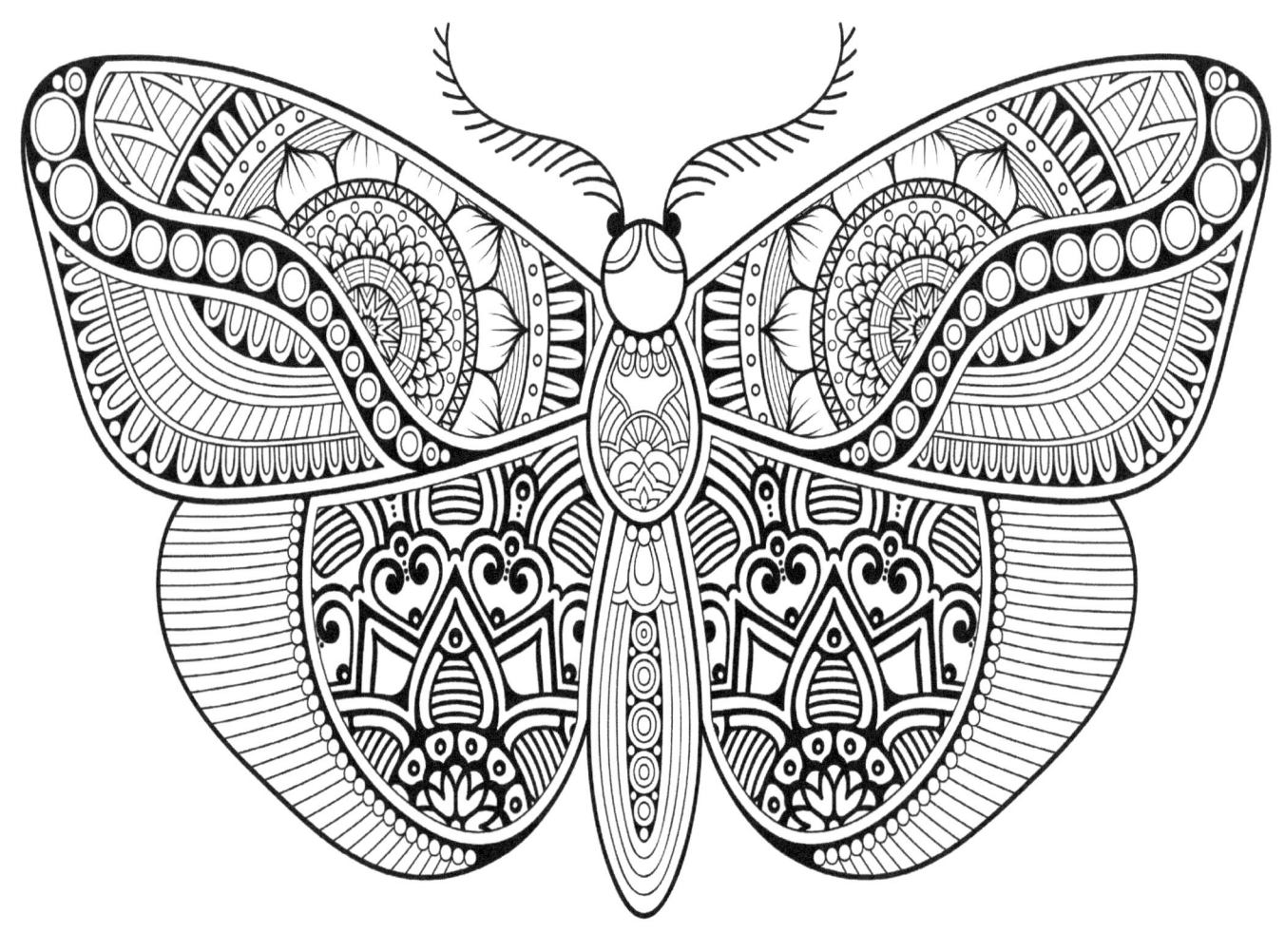

African Monarch Feed On The Milkweed Plant And Retain The Plant's Toxicity As They Mature Into Adults. Yes They Are Poisonous!

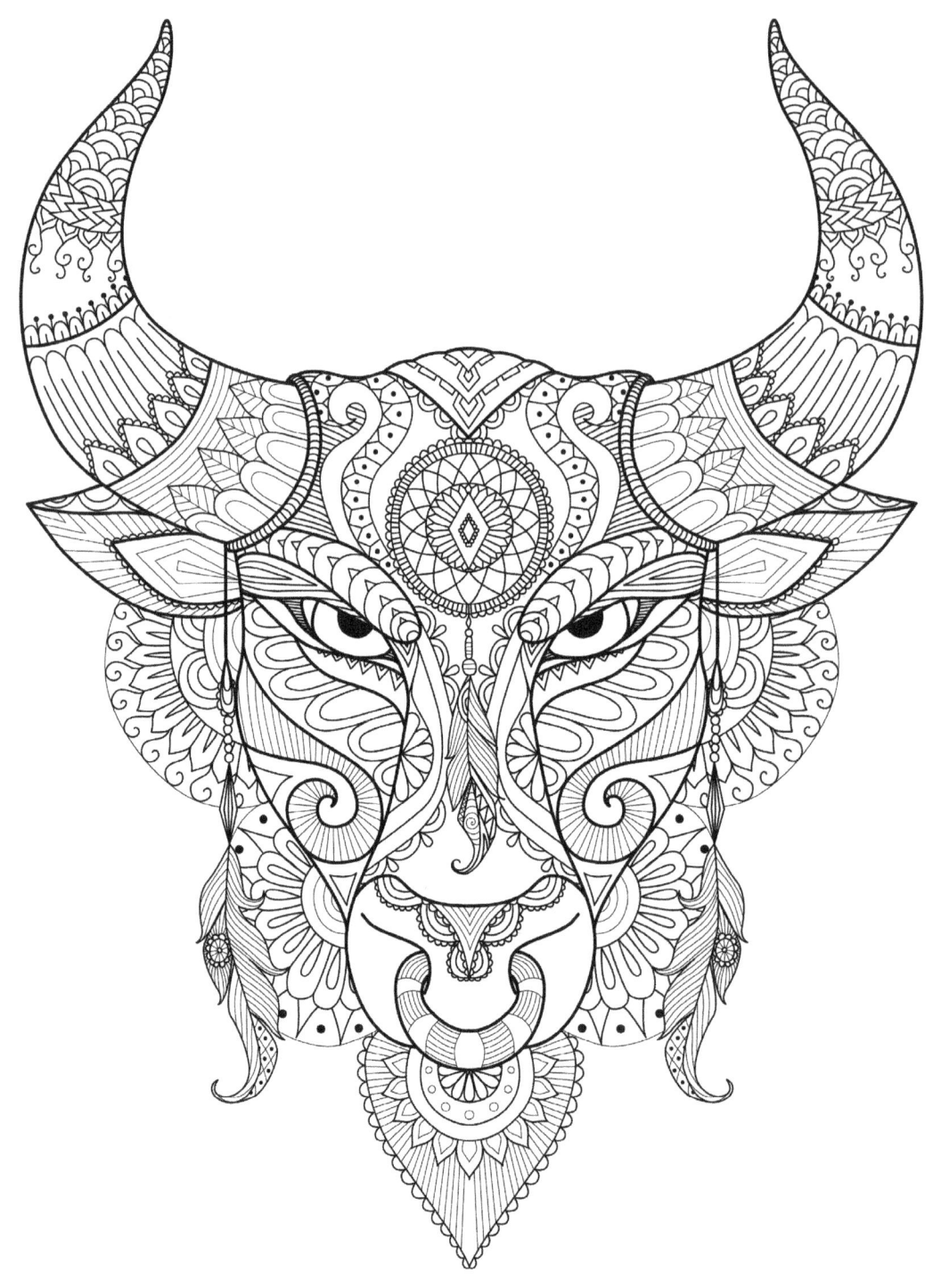

A Buffalo Never Forgives. They Have Been Known To Attack People That Have Harmed Them Even Years After The Event.

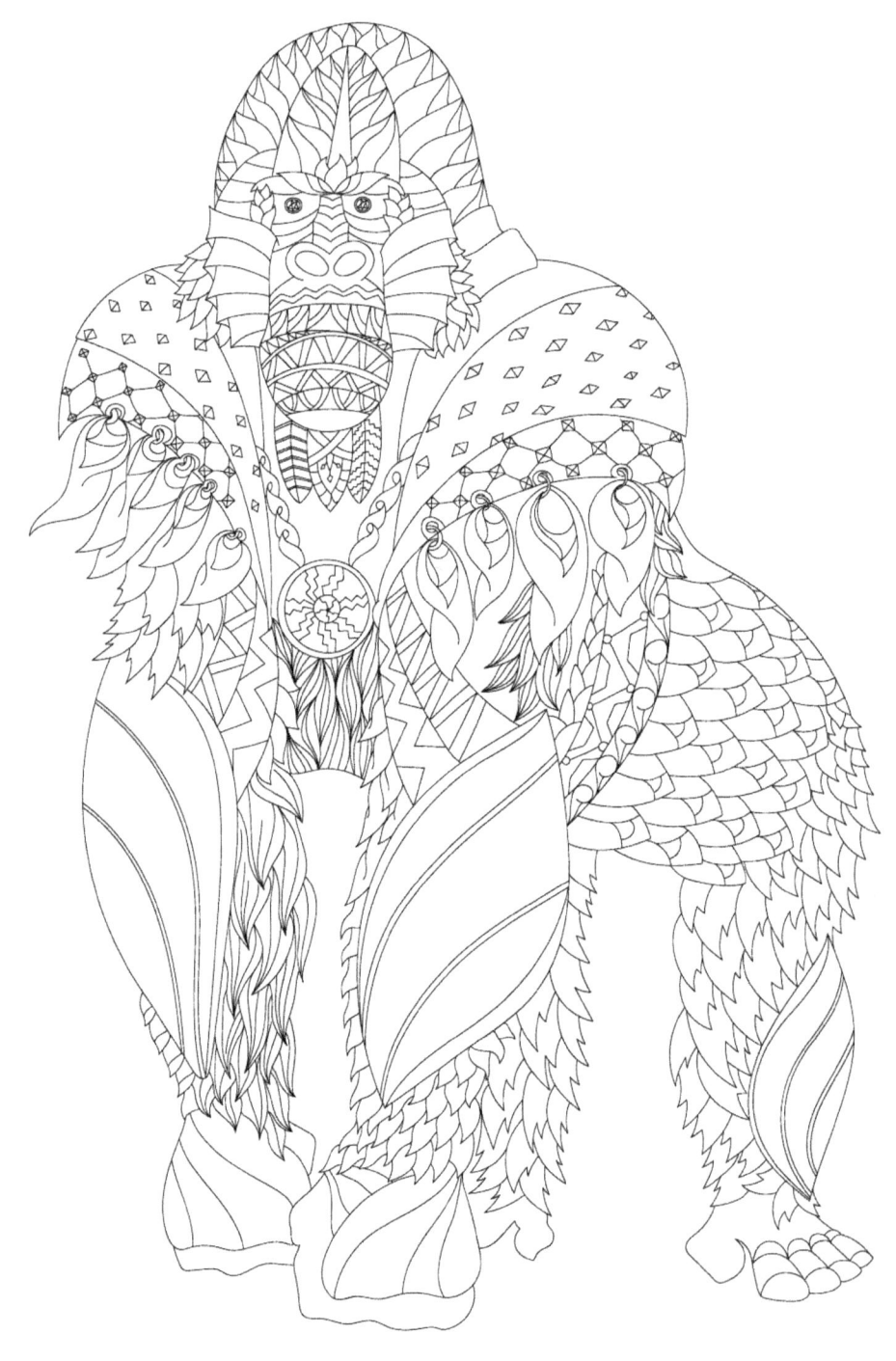

Gorillas Are Herbivores. They Spend Most Of Their Day Foraging For Bamboo

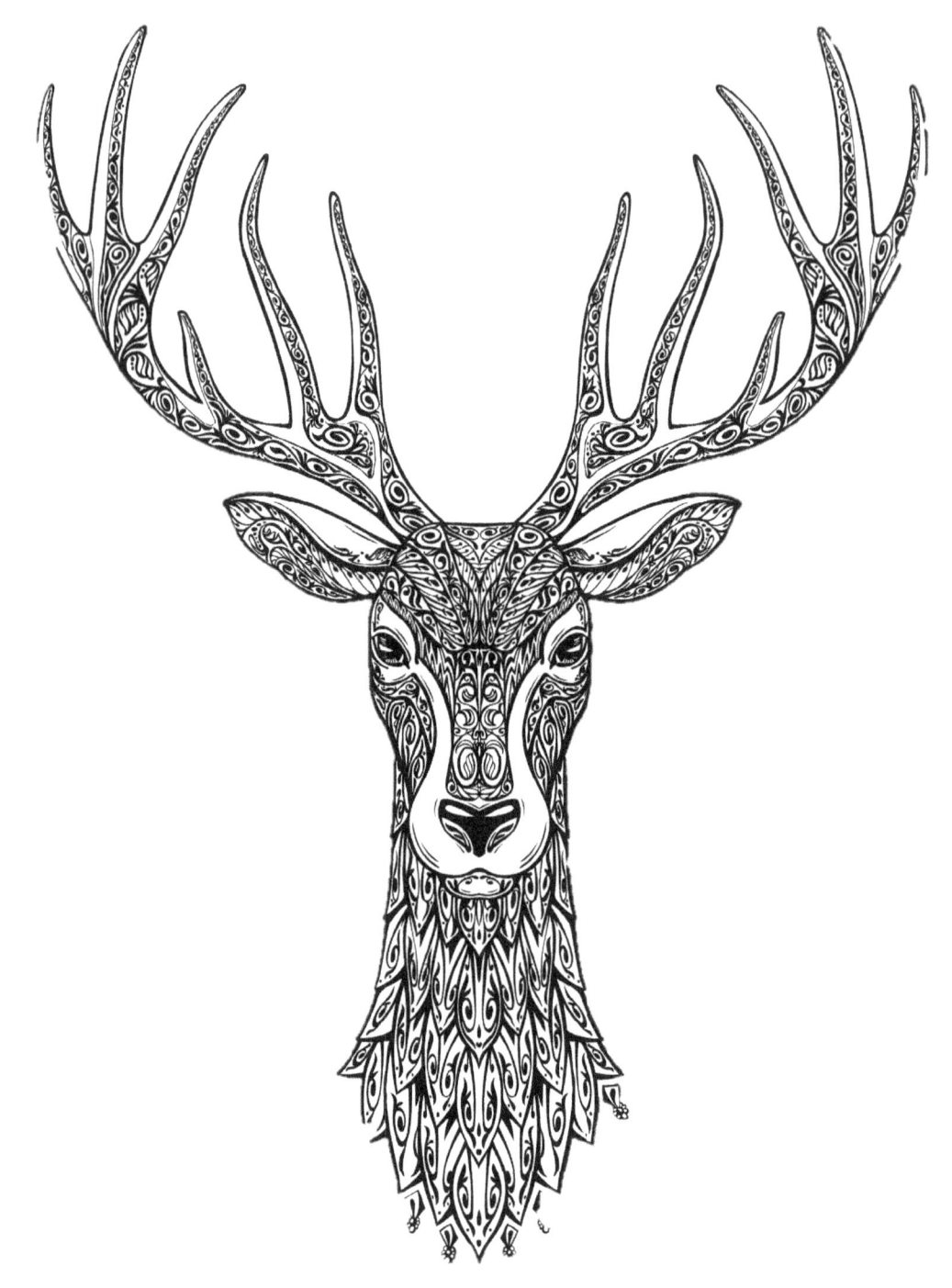

Only The Stag Has Antlers That Grow In Spring And Are Shed Every Year

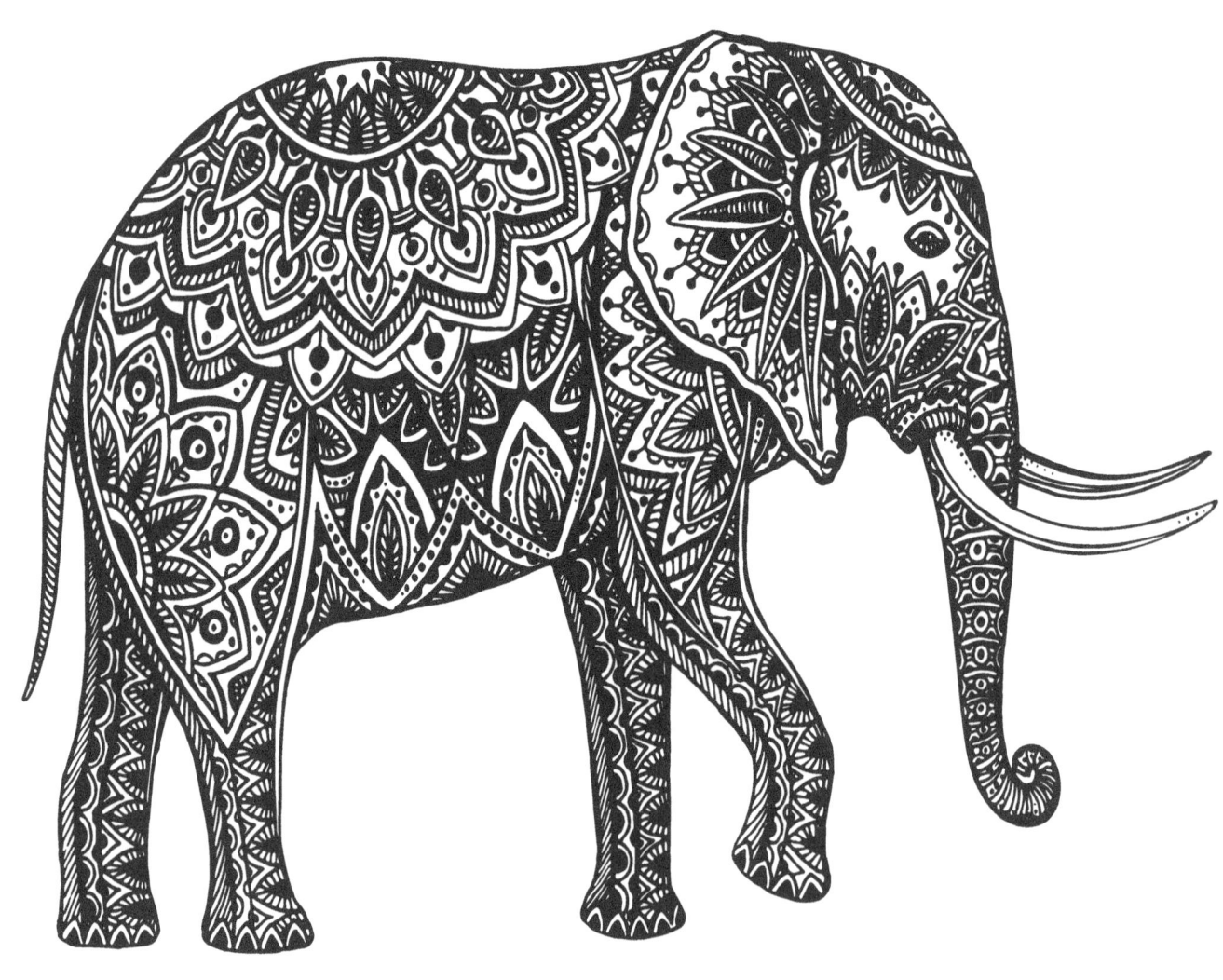

Did You Know Elephants can swim , They Use Their Trunk To Breathe Like A Snorkel In Deepwater

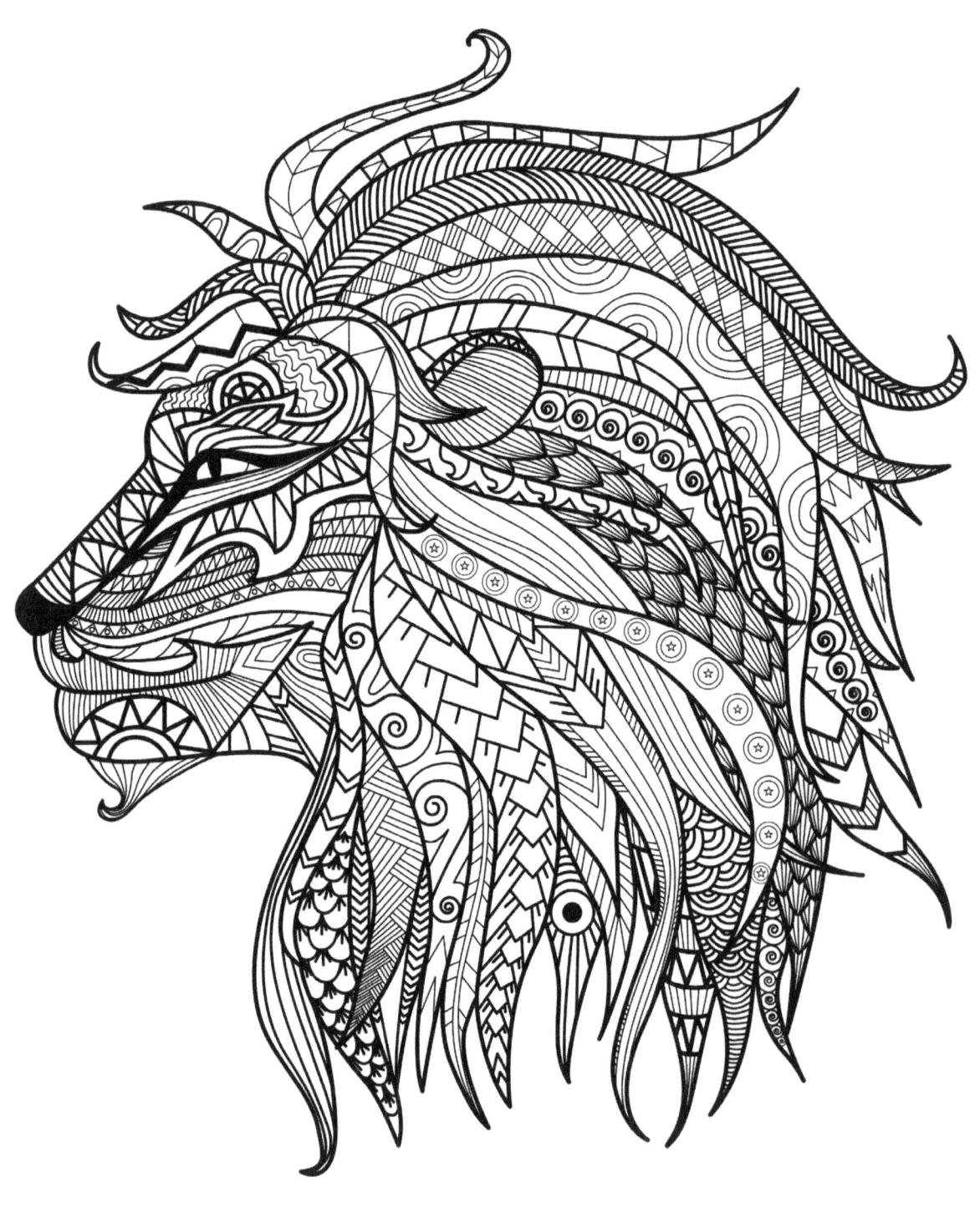

Lions Sleep Mostly In The Day For Up To 20 Hours

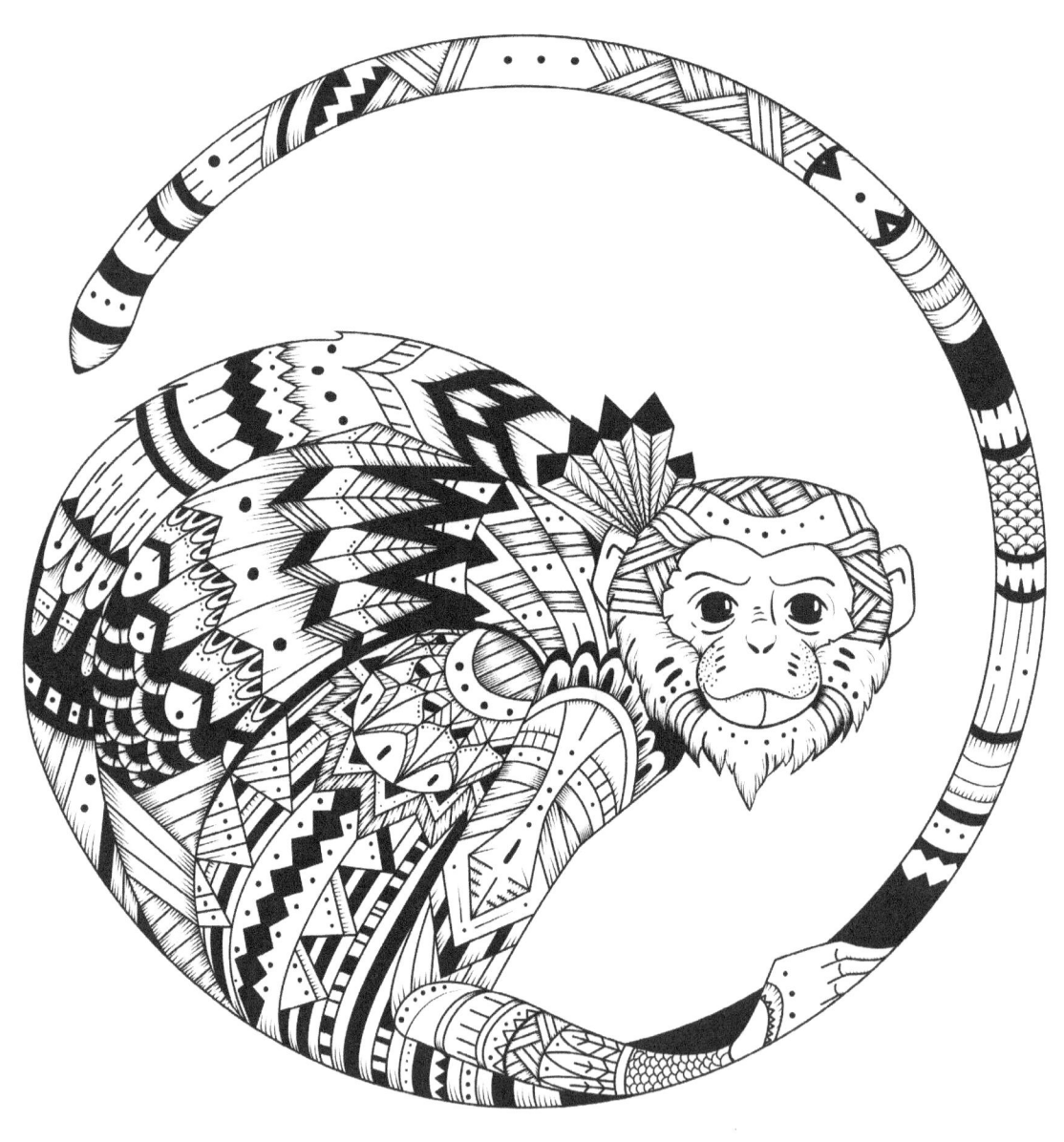

Vervet Monkey Spends Almost Entire Life On The Trees

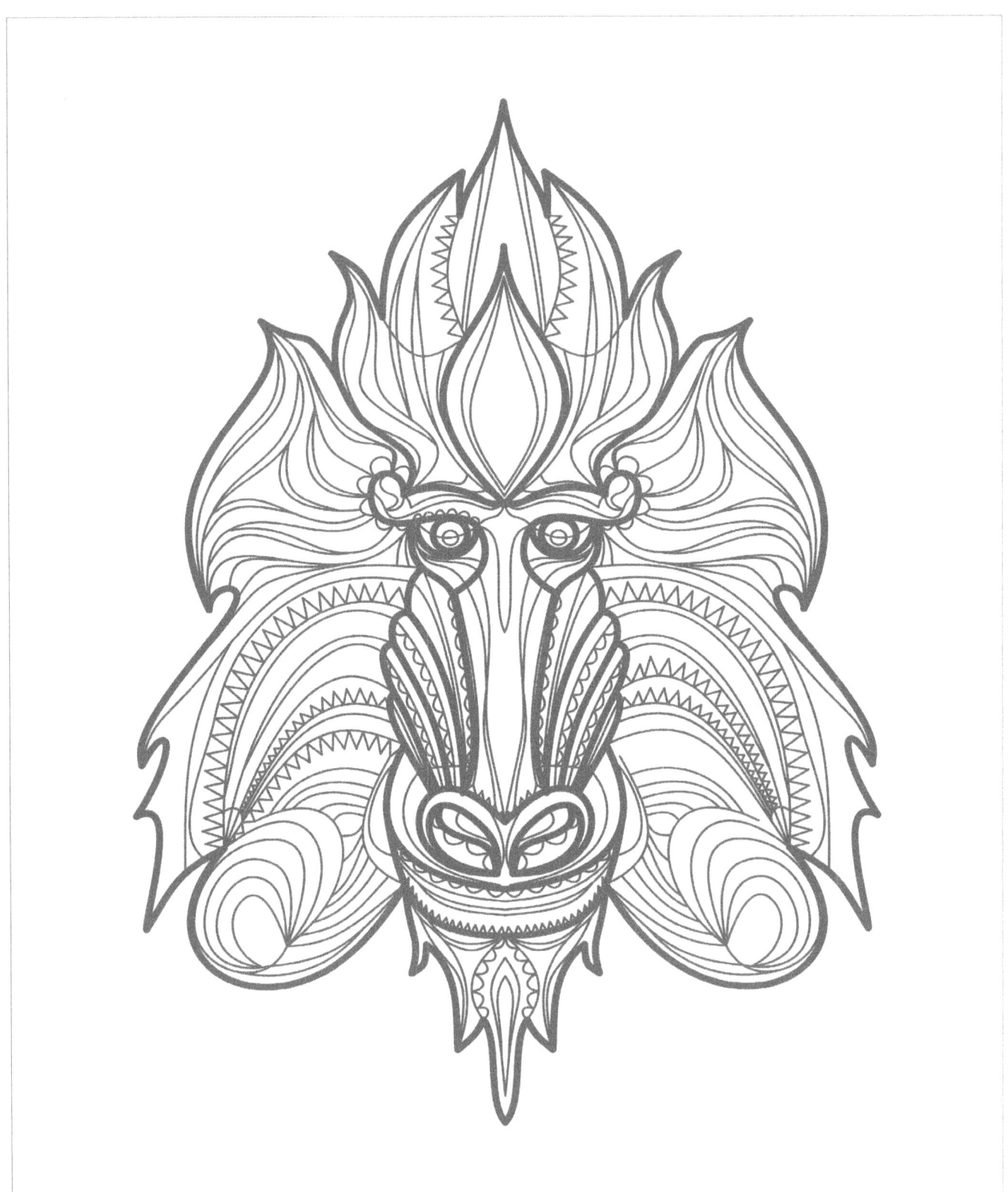

Baboons Have Over 30 Different Sounds That They Make To Communicate.

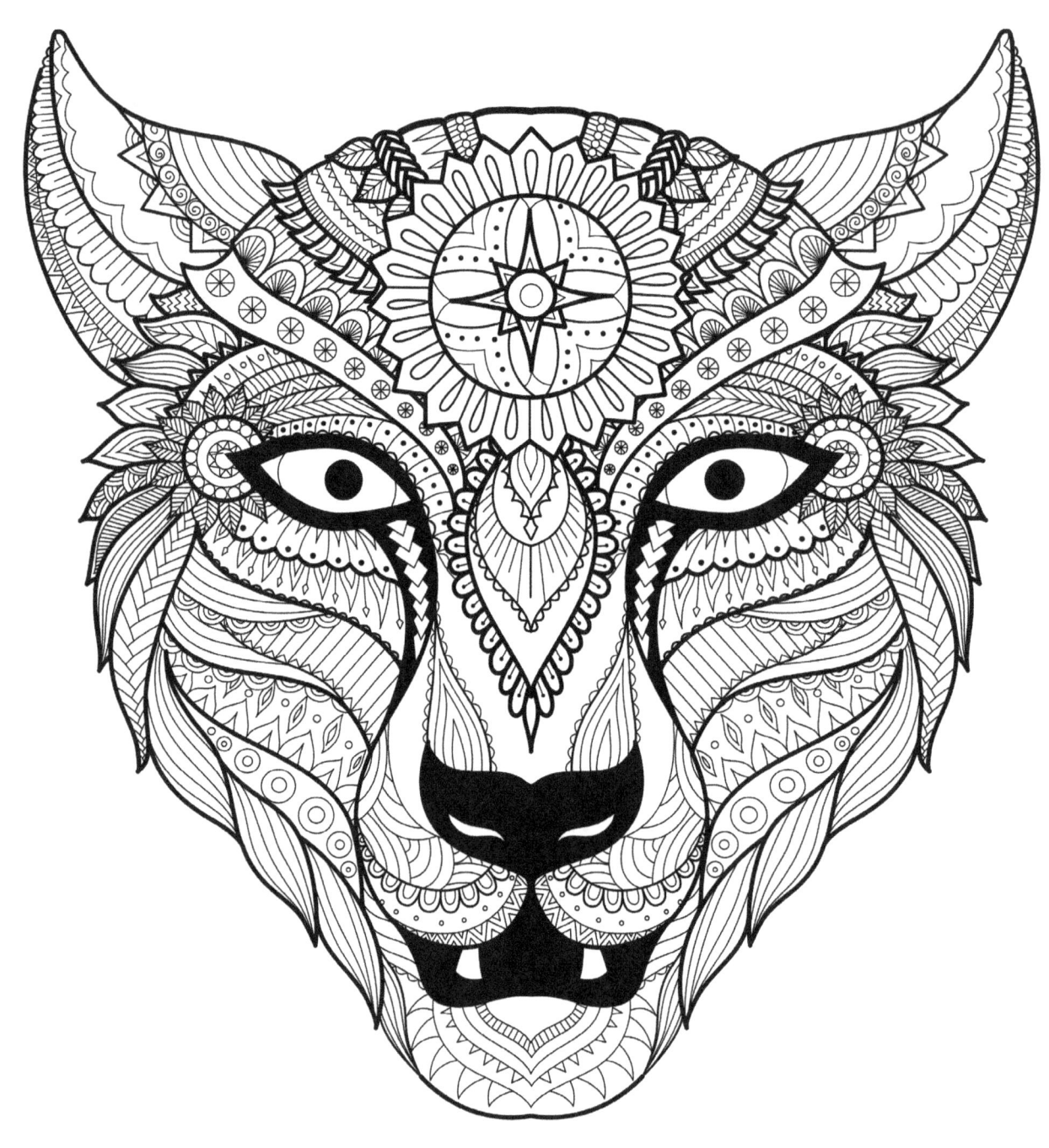

The Cheetah's Fur Is Covered In Solid Black Spots, And So Is Their Skin! The Black Fur Actually Grows Out Of The Black Spots On Their Skin.

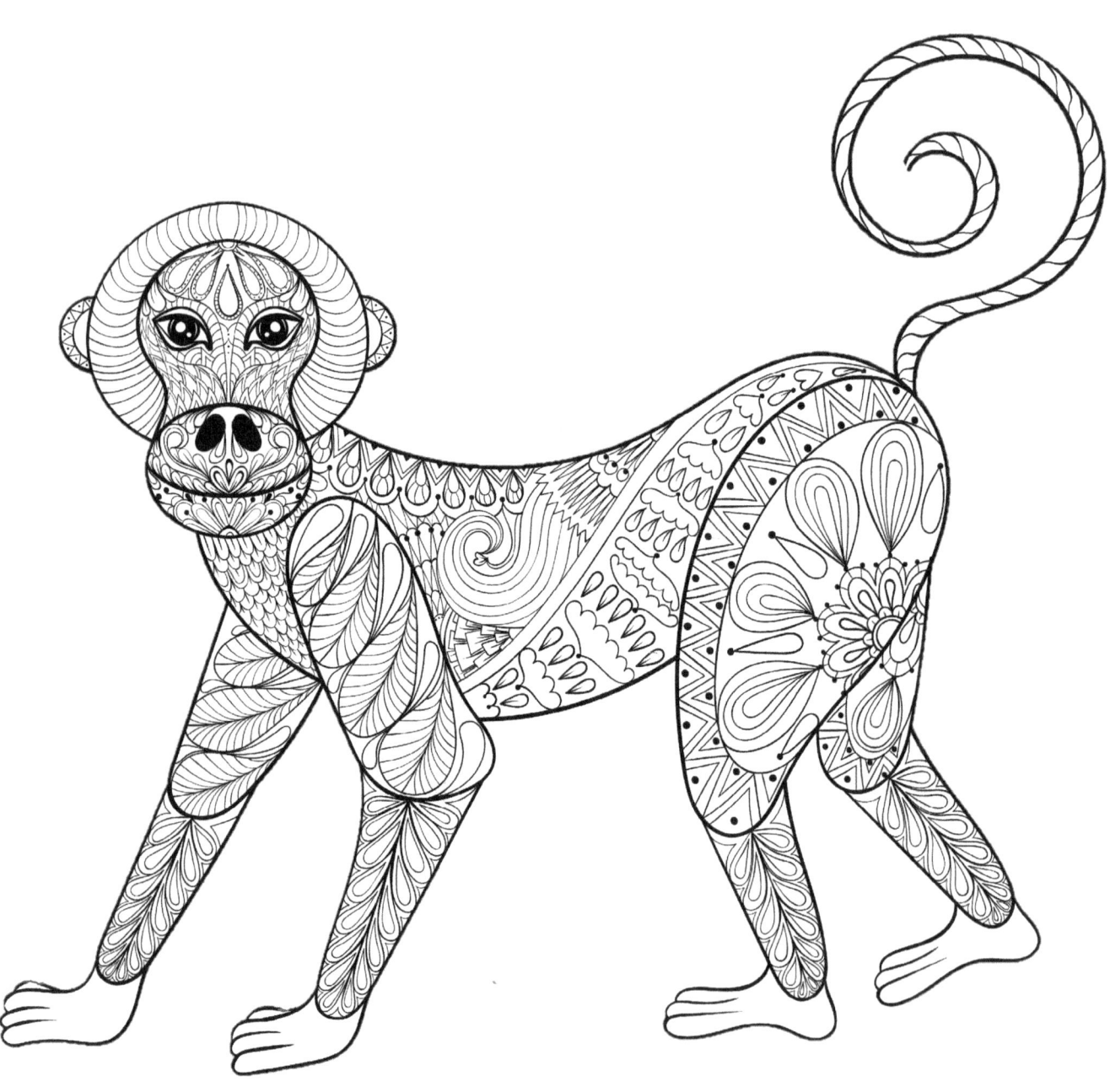

Mangabeys are some of the most rare and endangered monkeys on Earth. These large forest dwellers are found only in Africa.

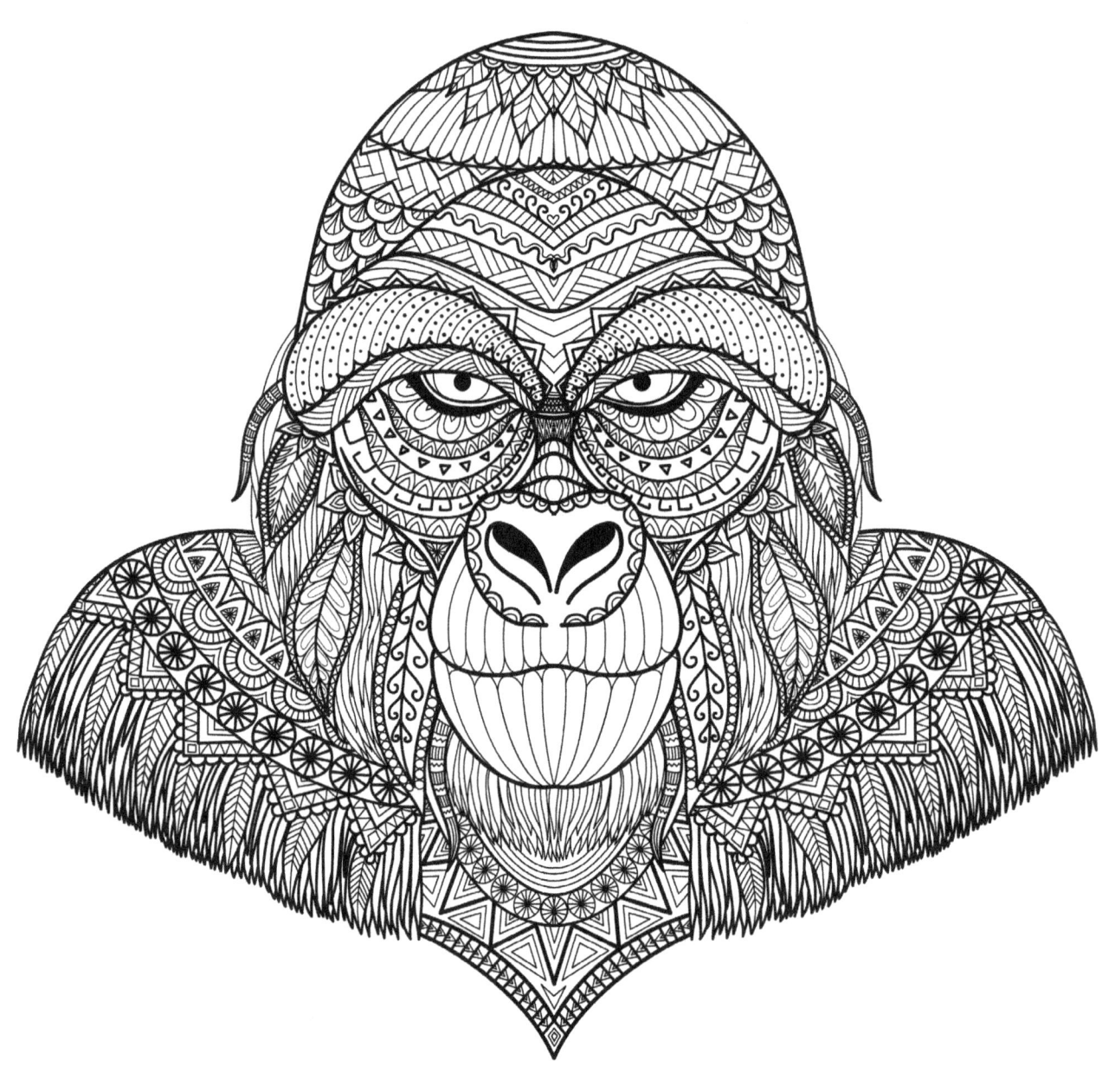

Gorillas stick to a mainly vegetarian diet, feeding on stems, bamboo shoots and fruits.

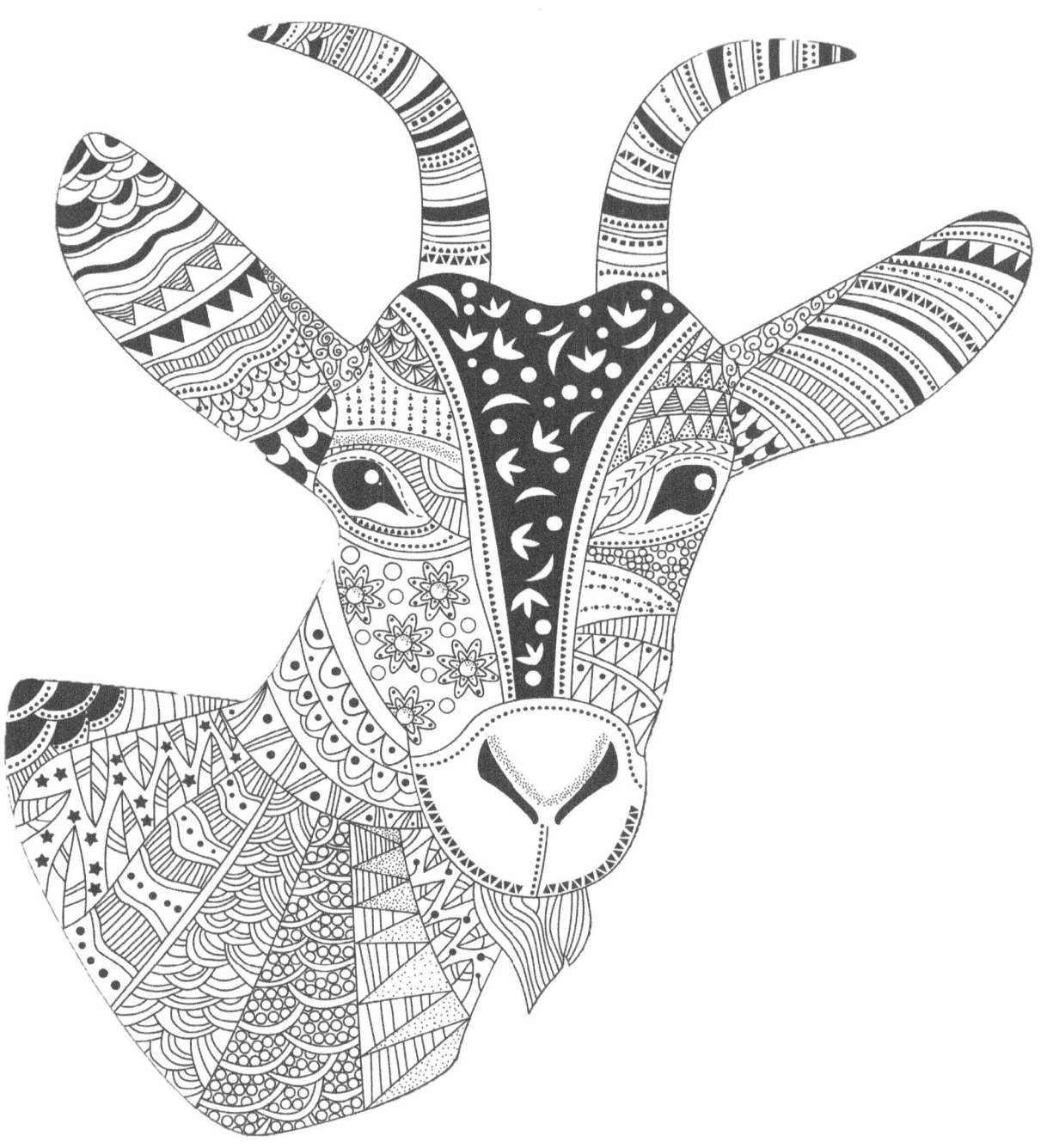

The Pygmy Goat is a species that has been domesticated. This is a small species. The females can be about 16 inches tall and the males are about 23 inches tall

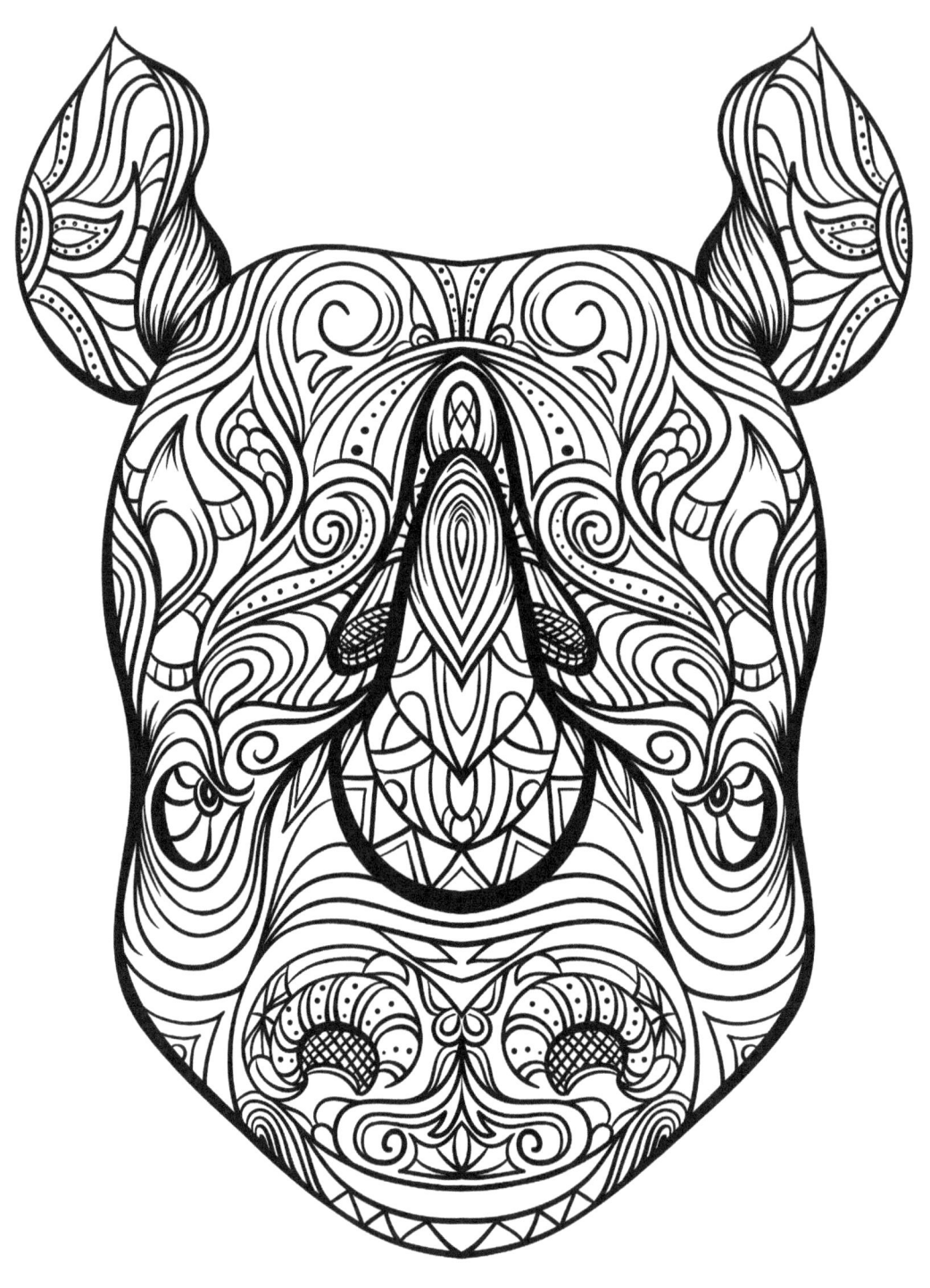

Rhinoceros are herbivores (plant eaters).

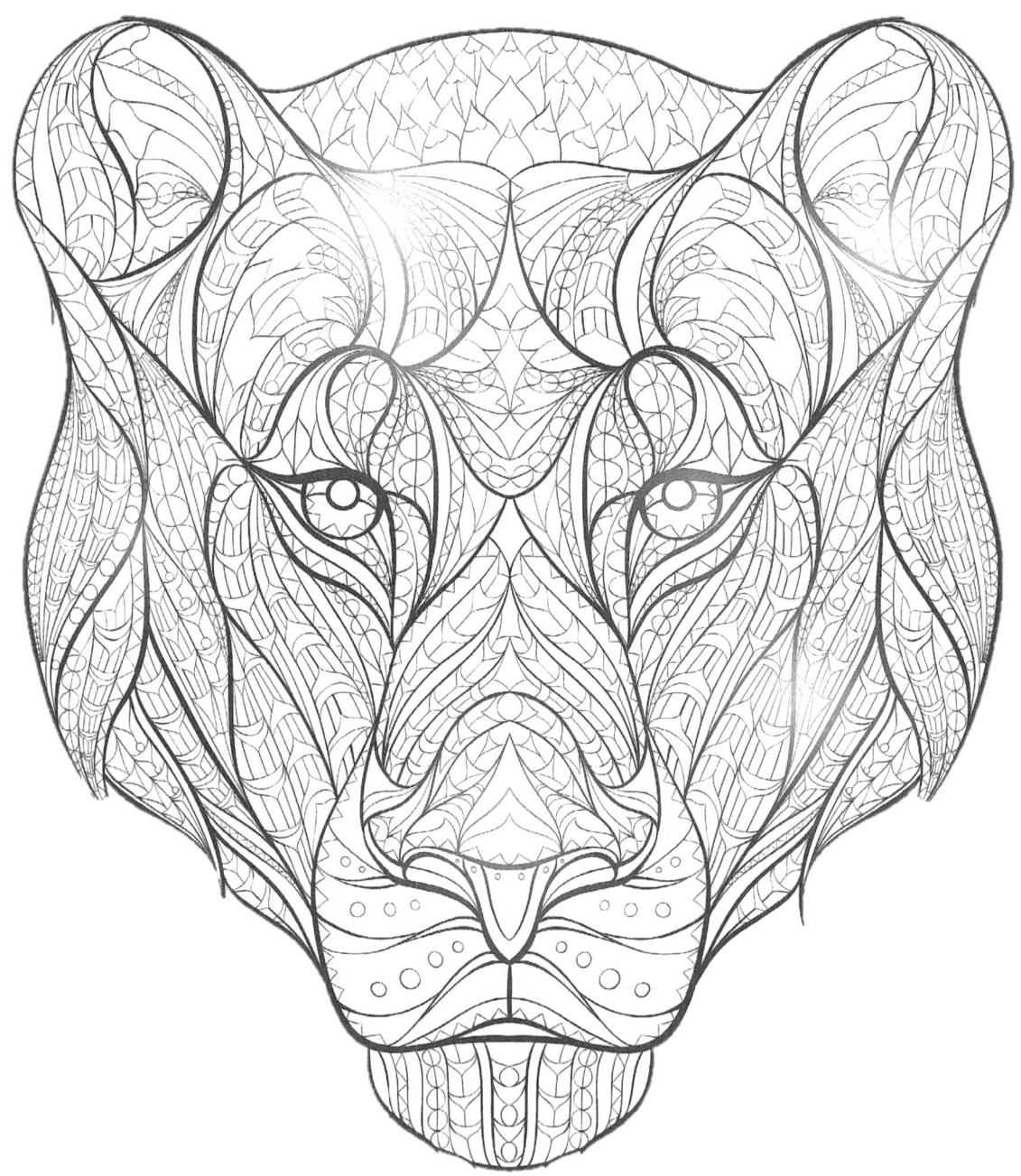

Female lions do the hunting and male lions are the first to eat food.

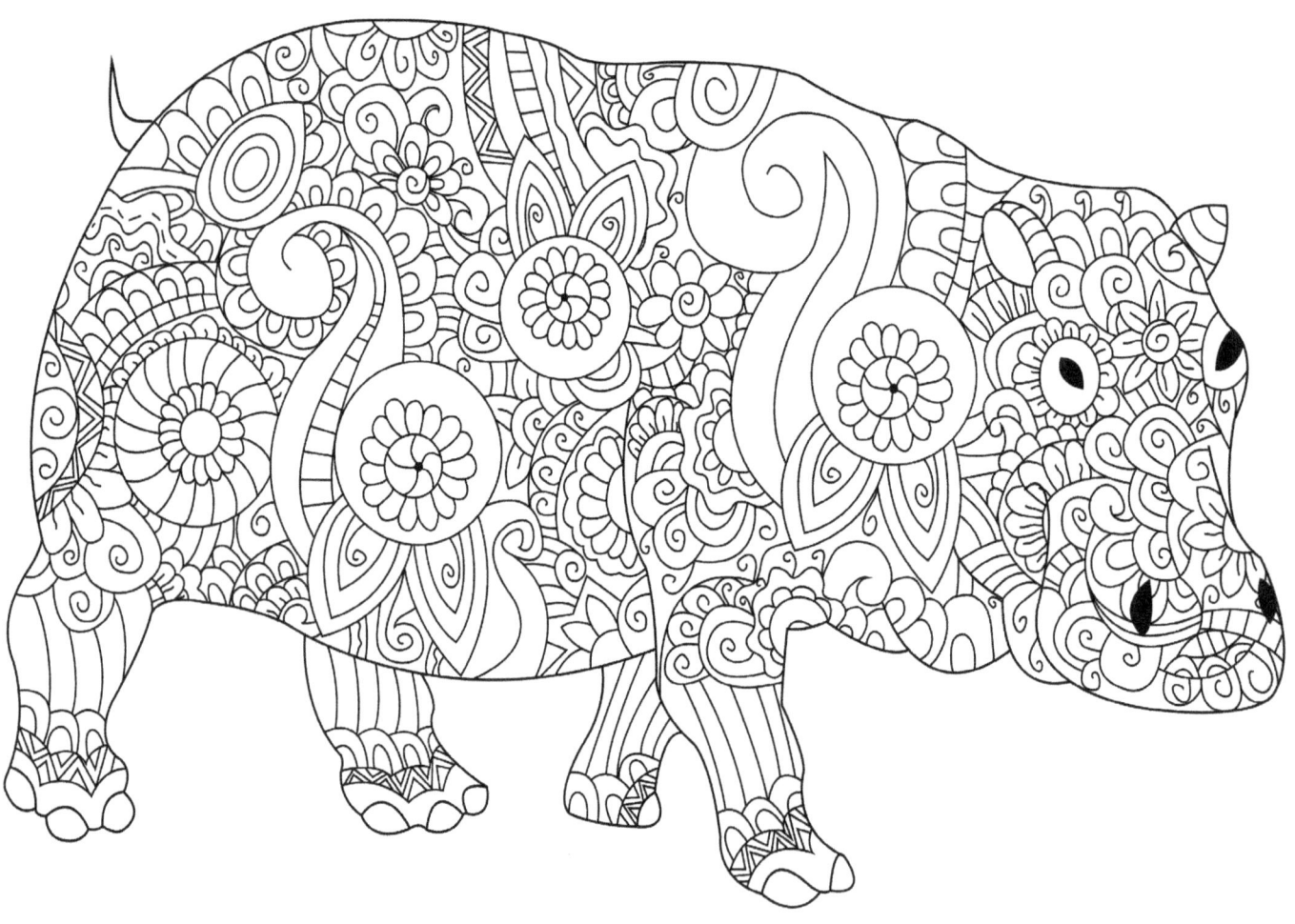

Hippos can't swim or float! They walk or stand on surfaces below the water like sandbanks

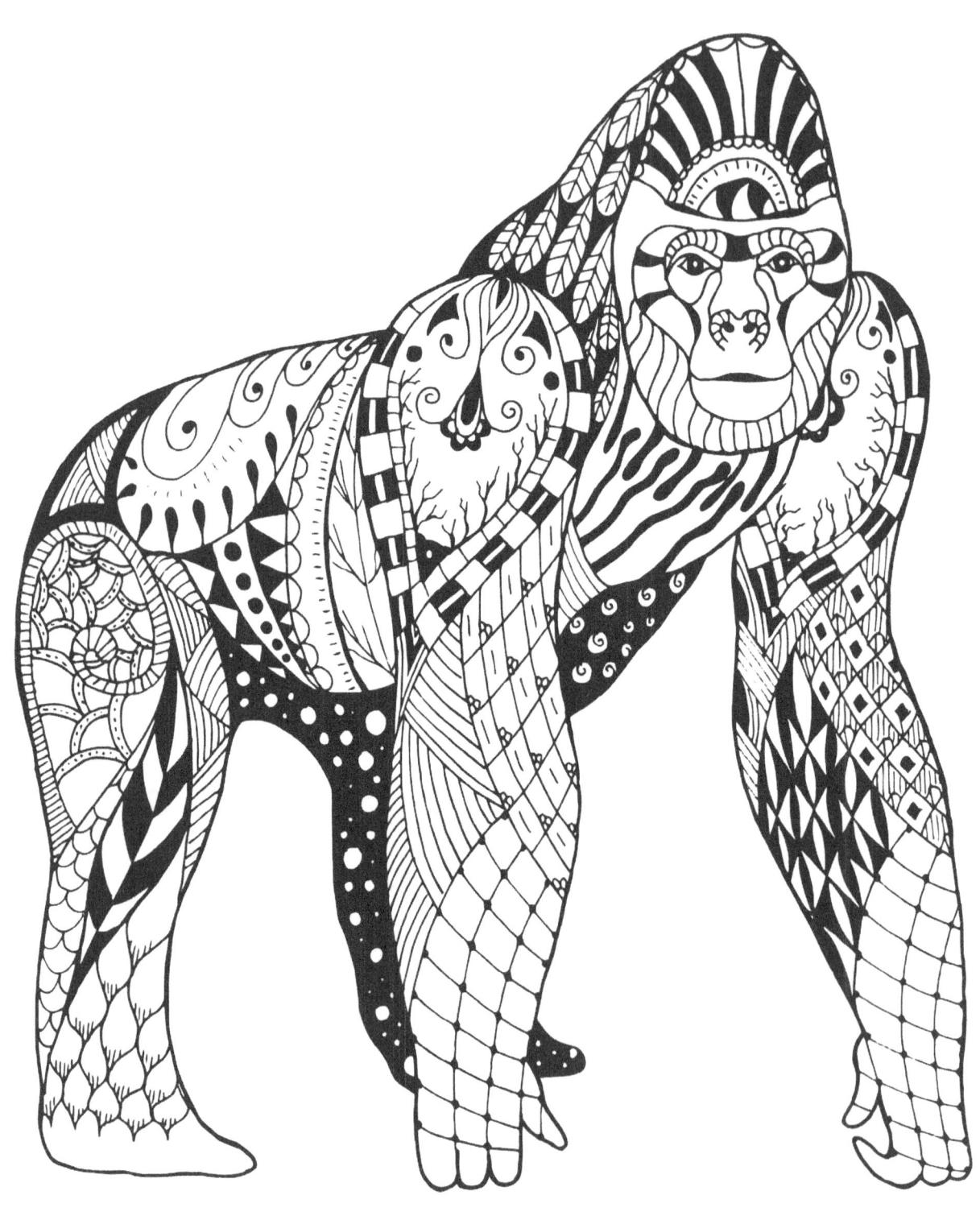

Mountain gorillas are as shy as they are strong.

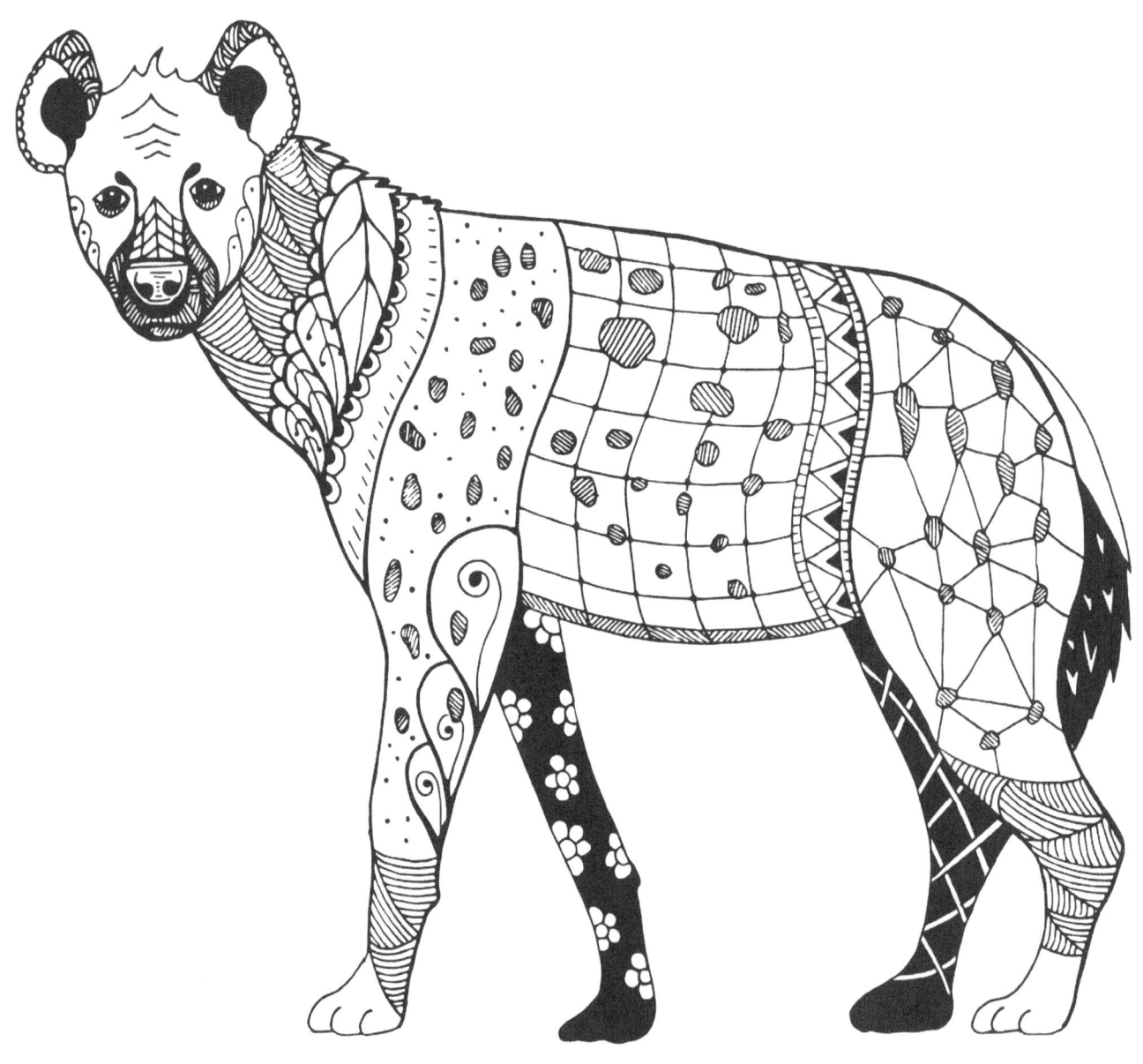

Female hyenas are more muscular and more aggressive than their male counterparts. This is because the females have three times as much testosterone in their bodies. As a result, spotted hyena societies are <u>matriarchal</u>. Even girl cubs rule over the boys.

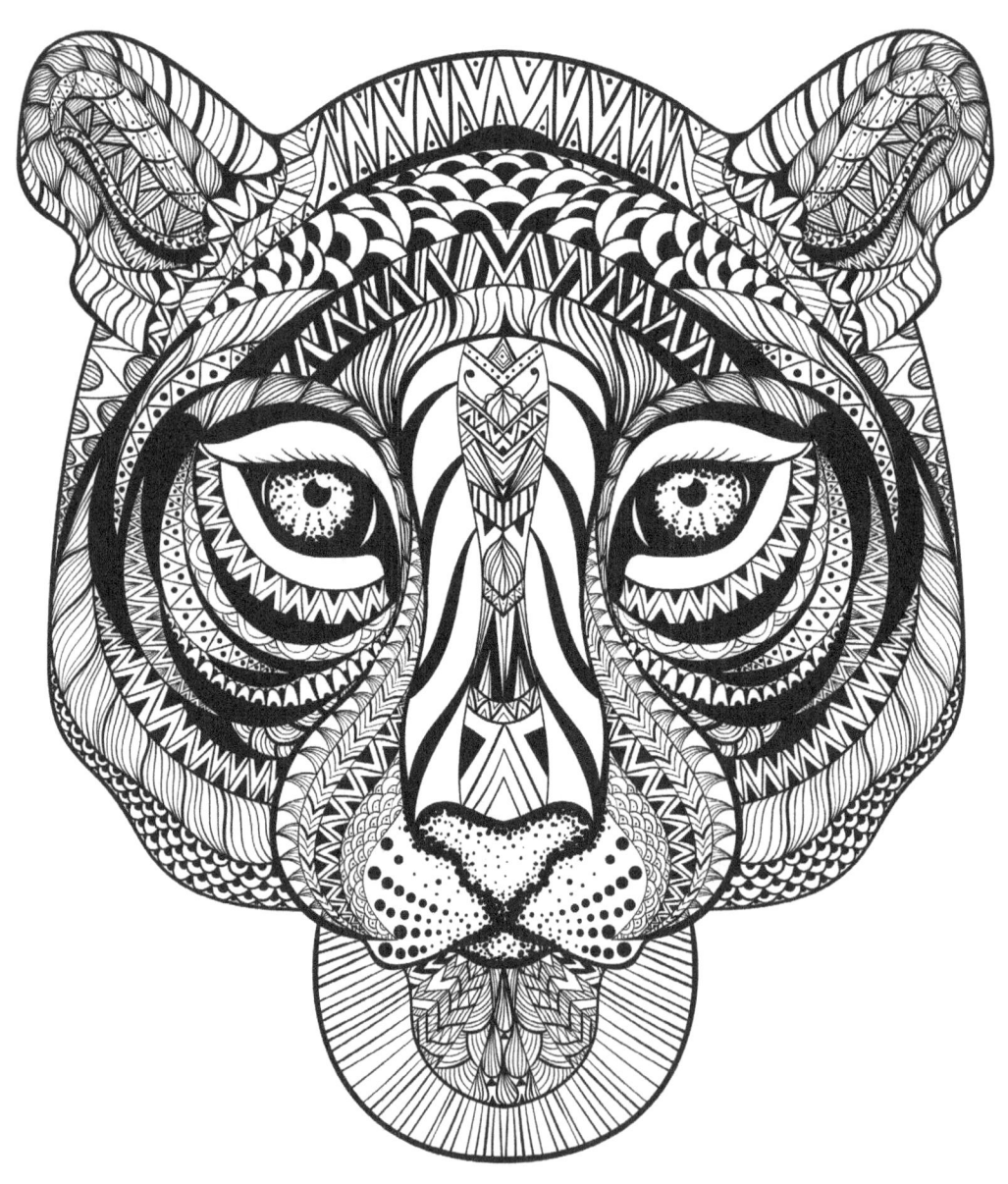

Though classified as a roaring cat, leopards usually bark when they have something to say.

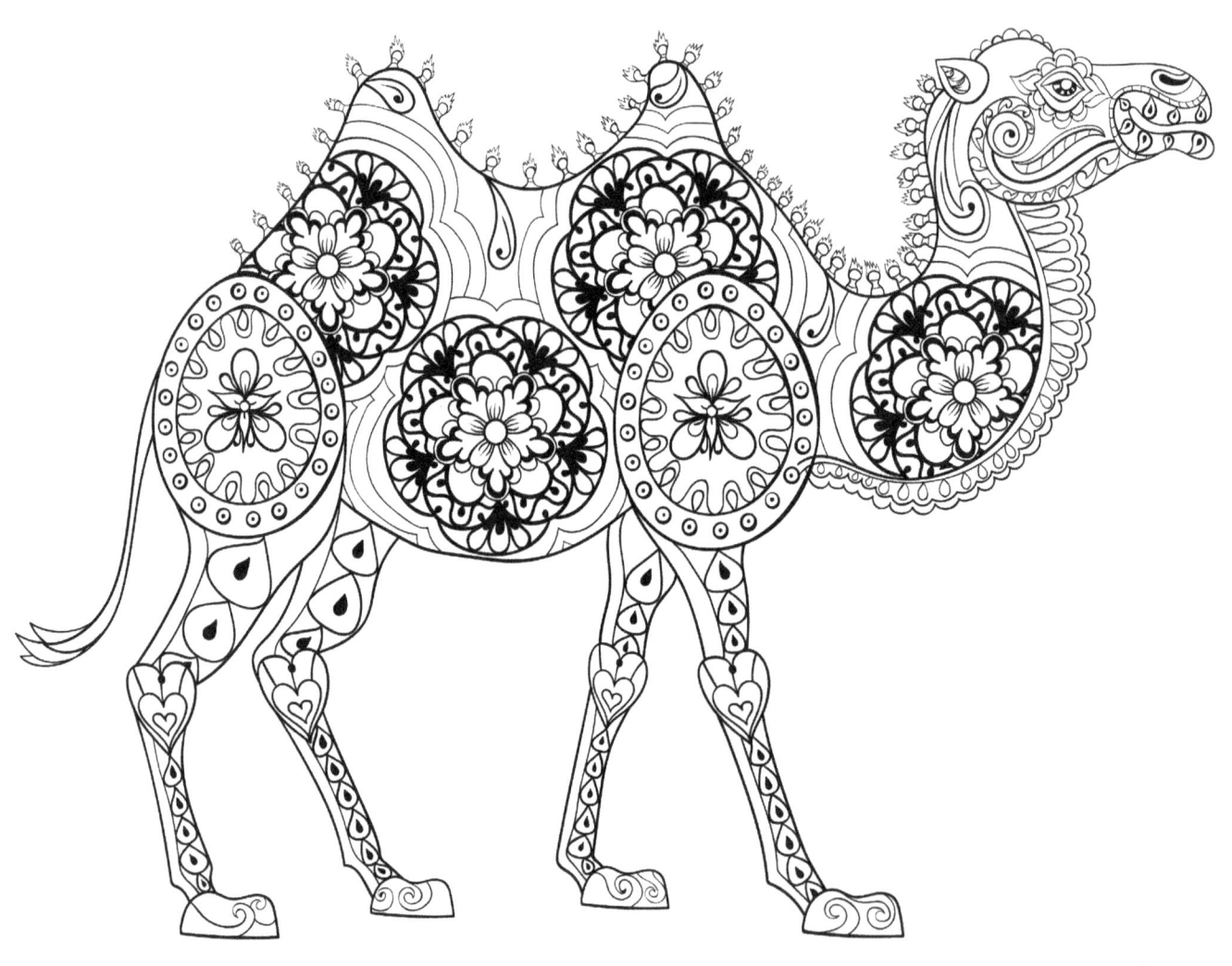

A camel's hump does not store water. Their humps store fat.

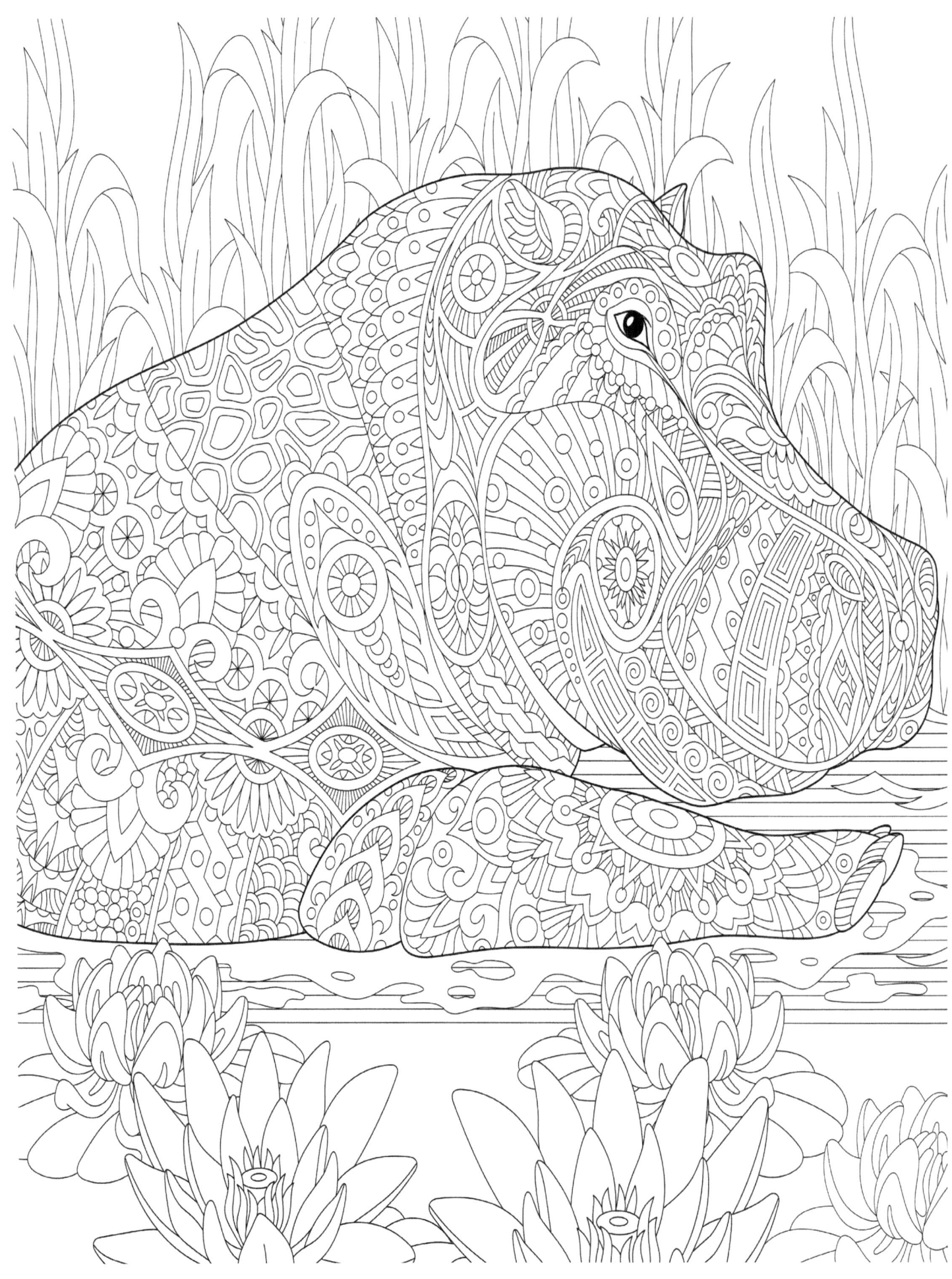

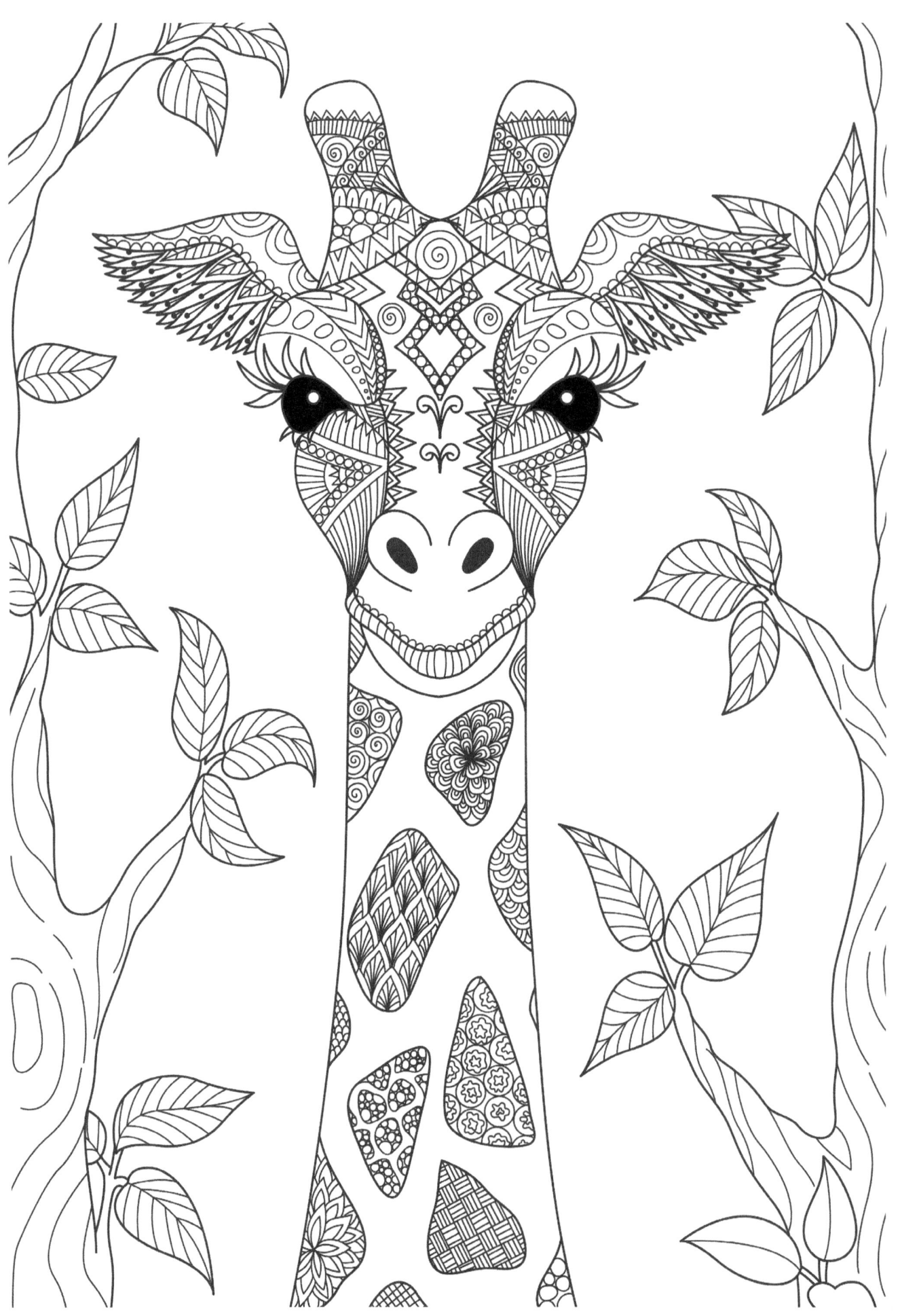

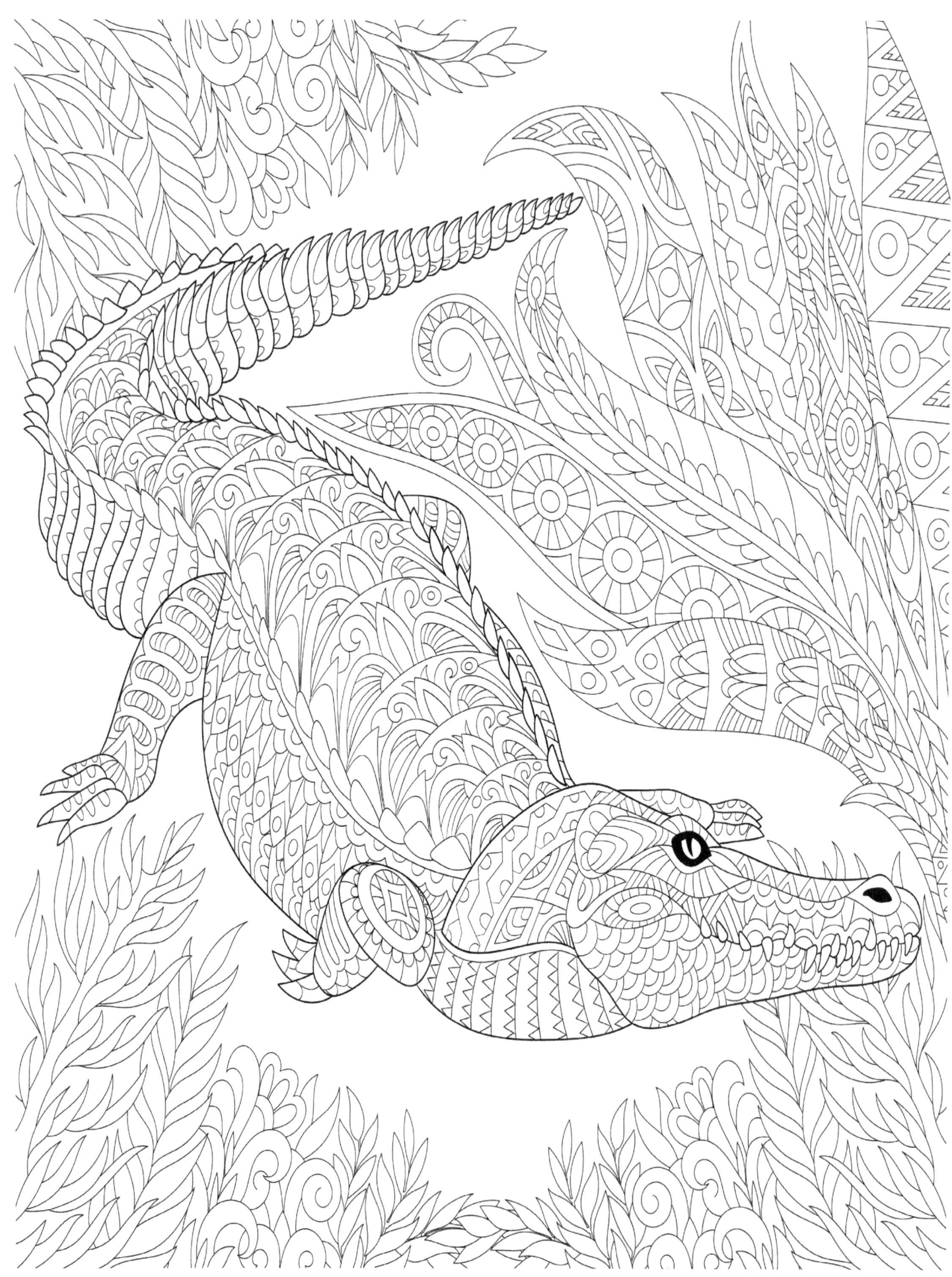

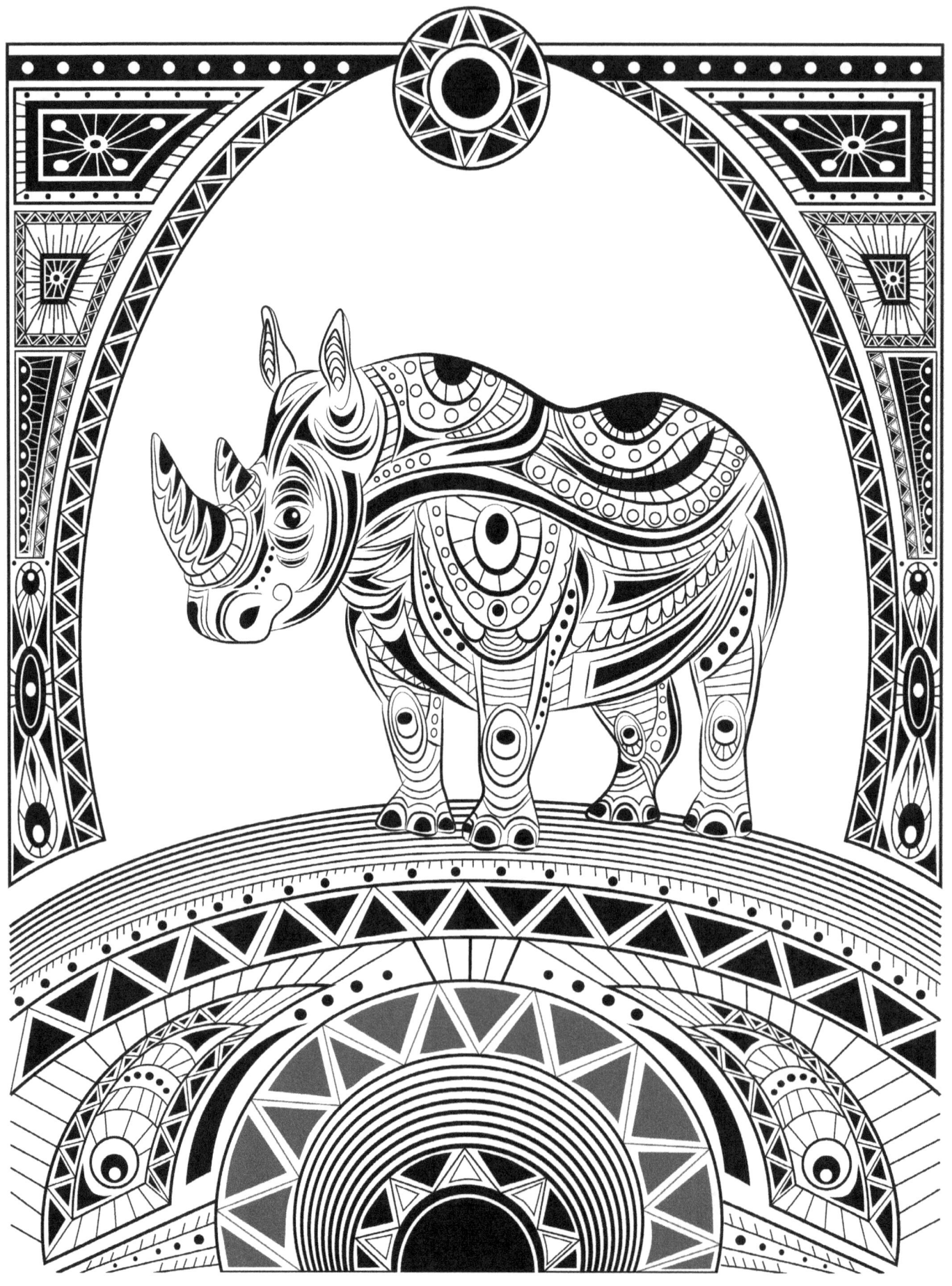

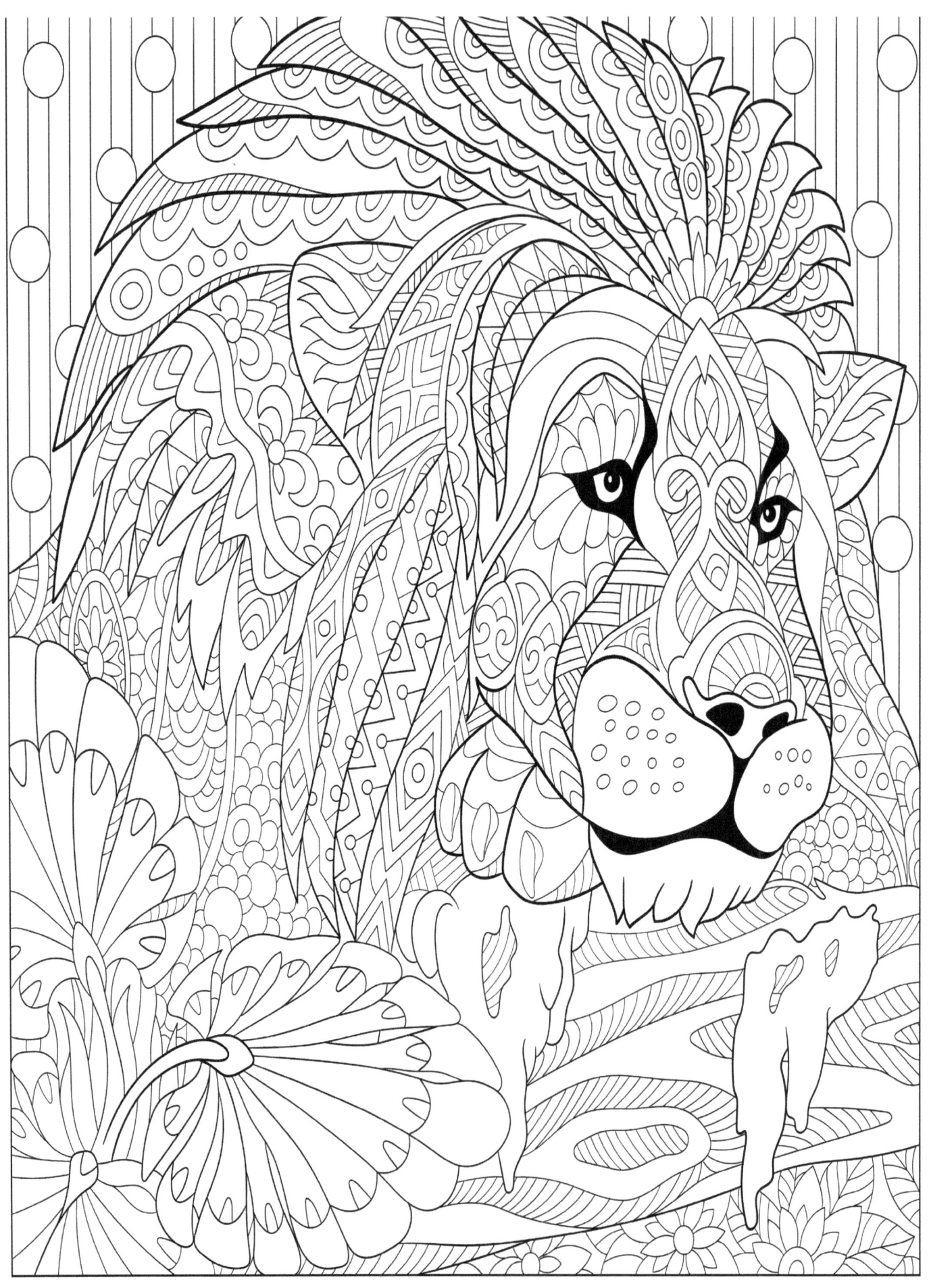

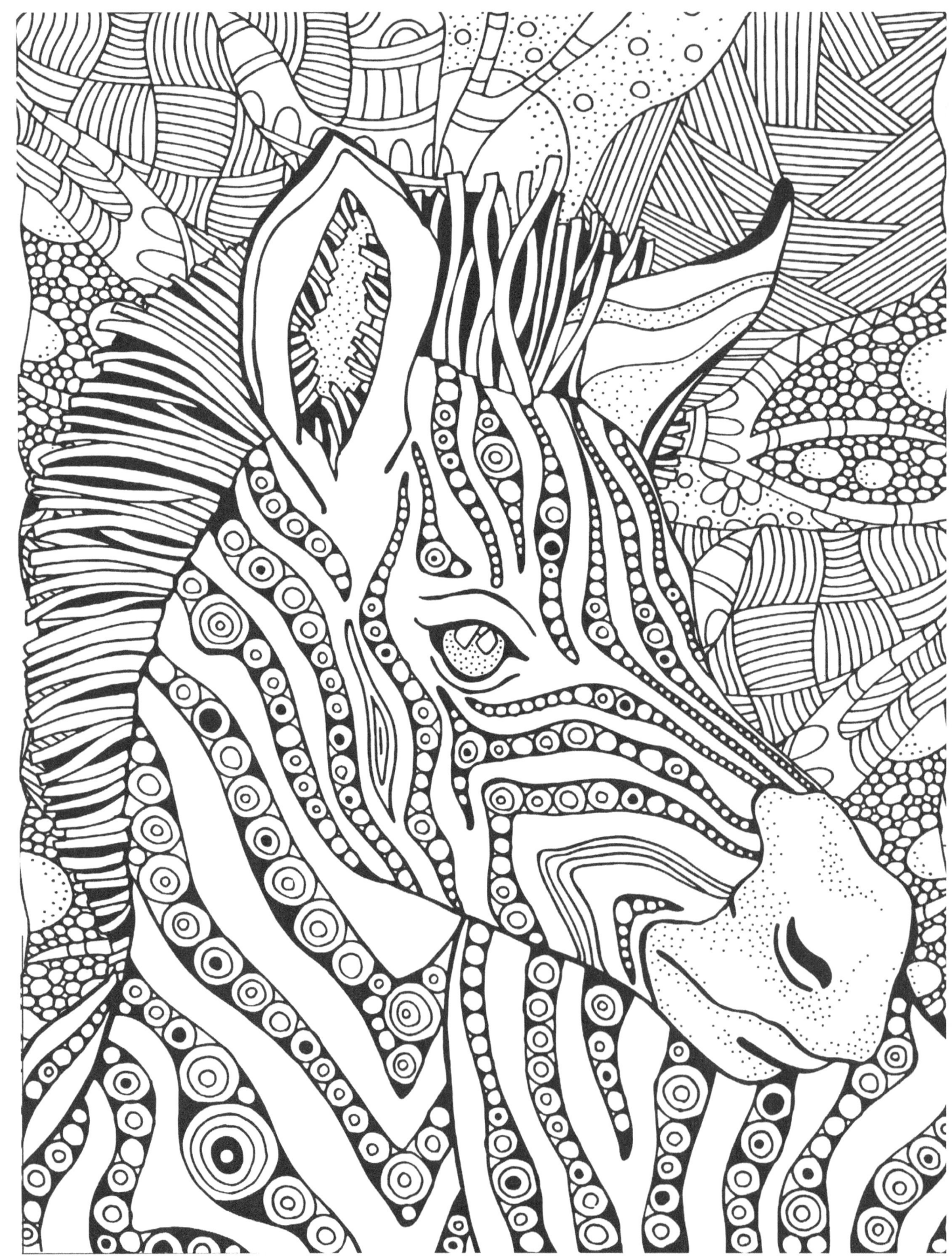

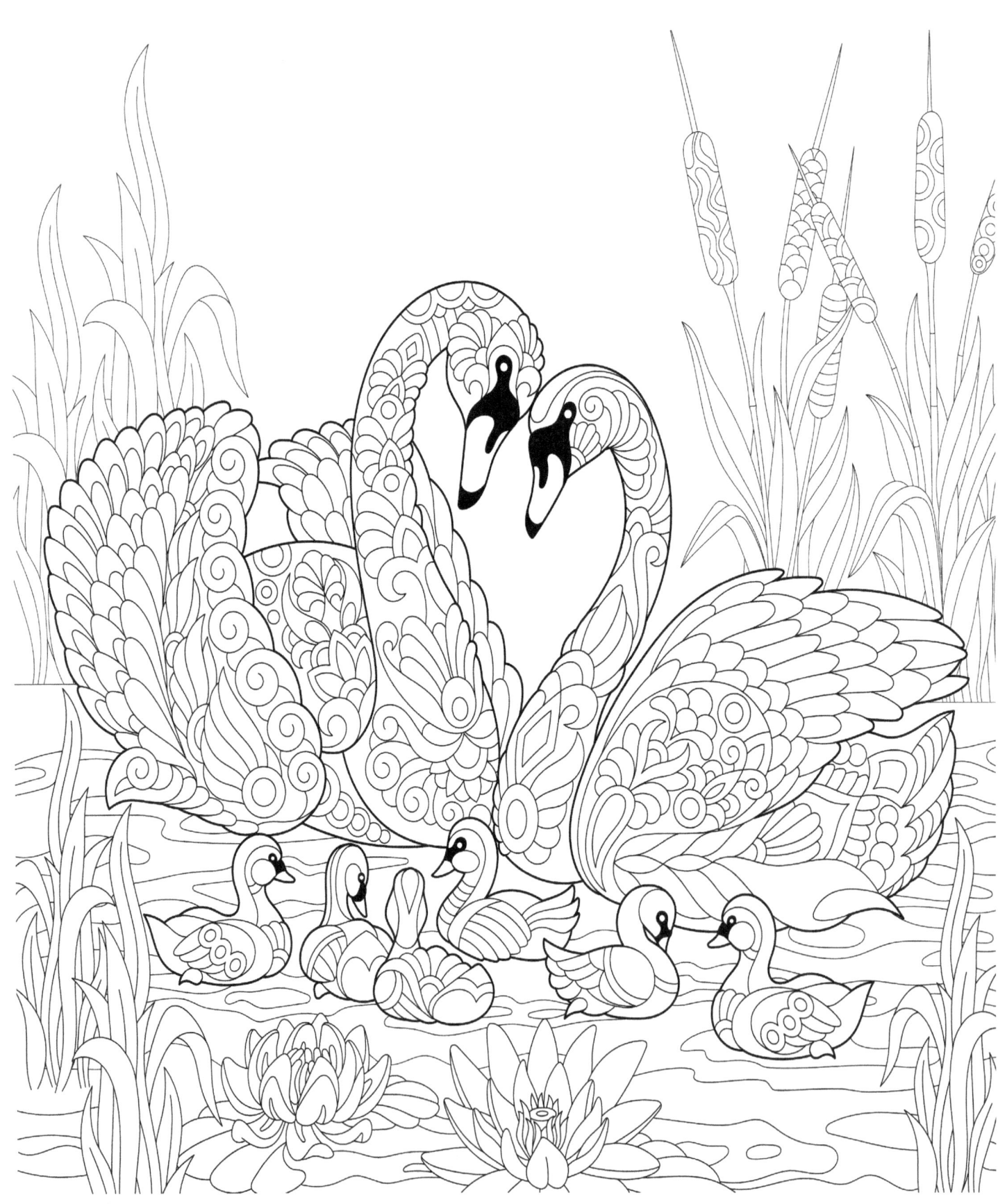

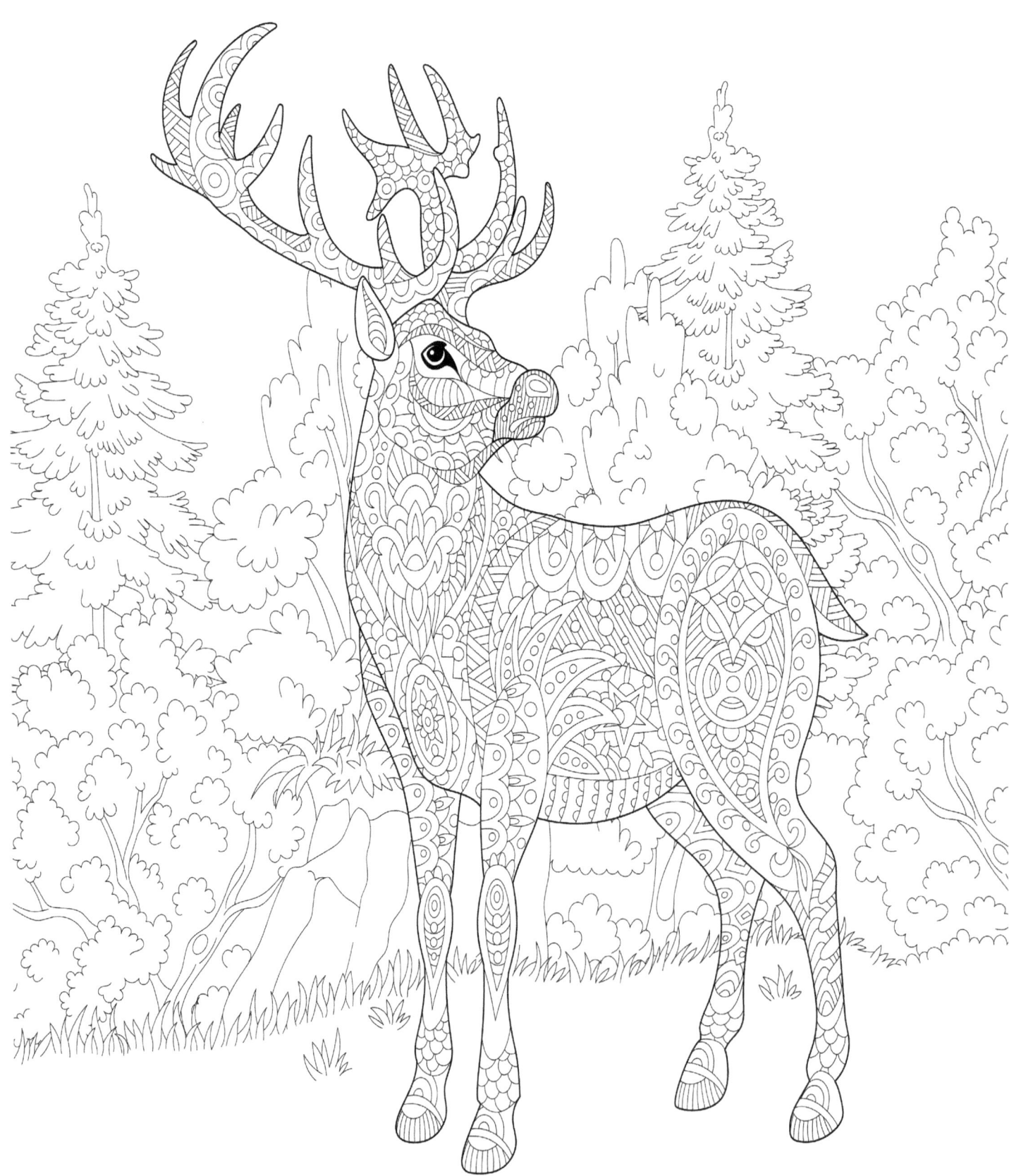

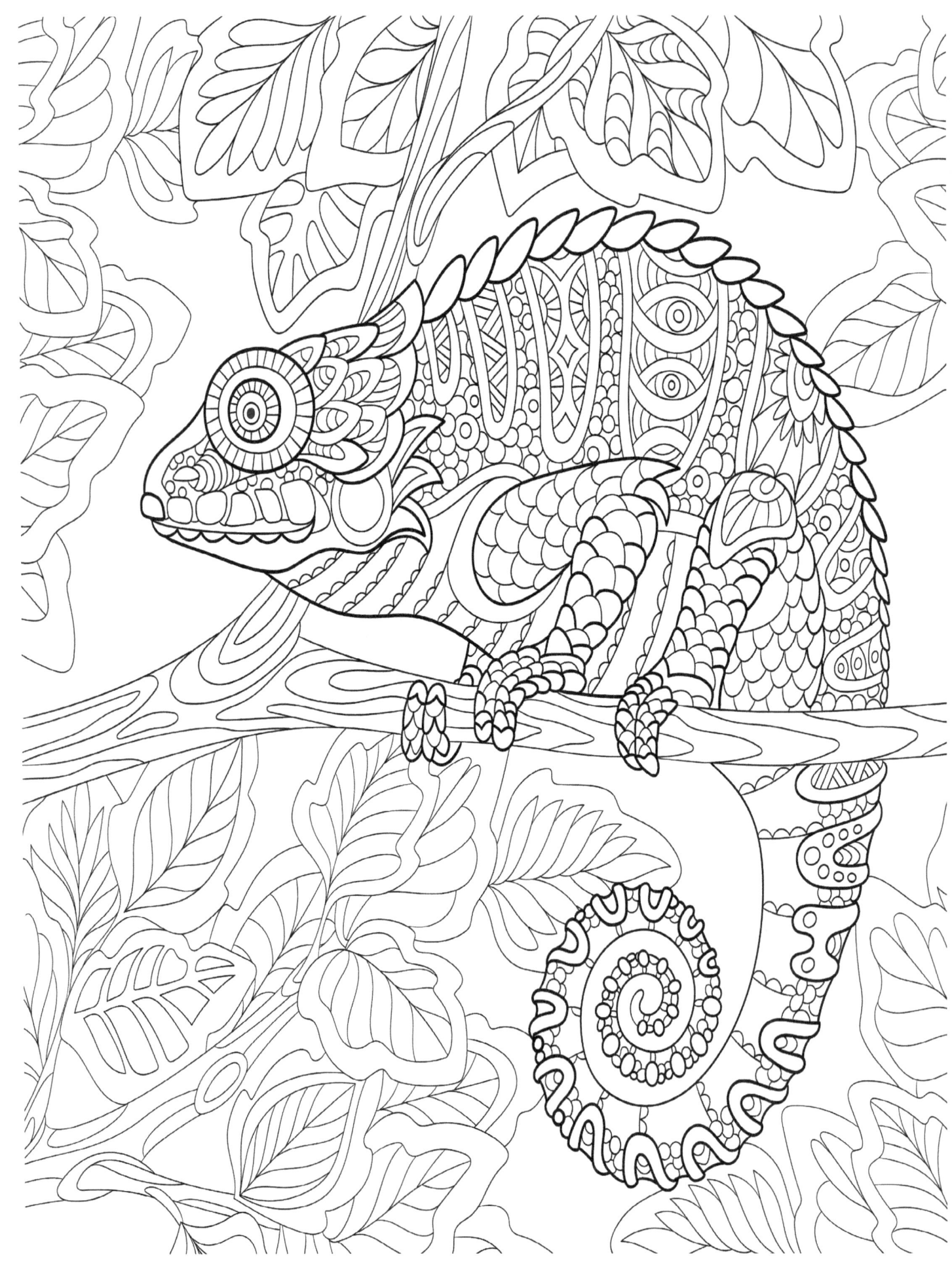

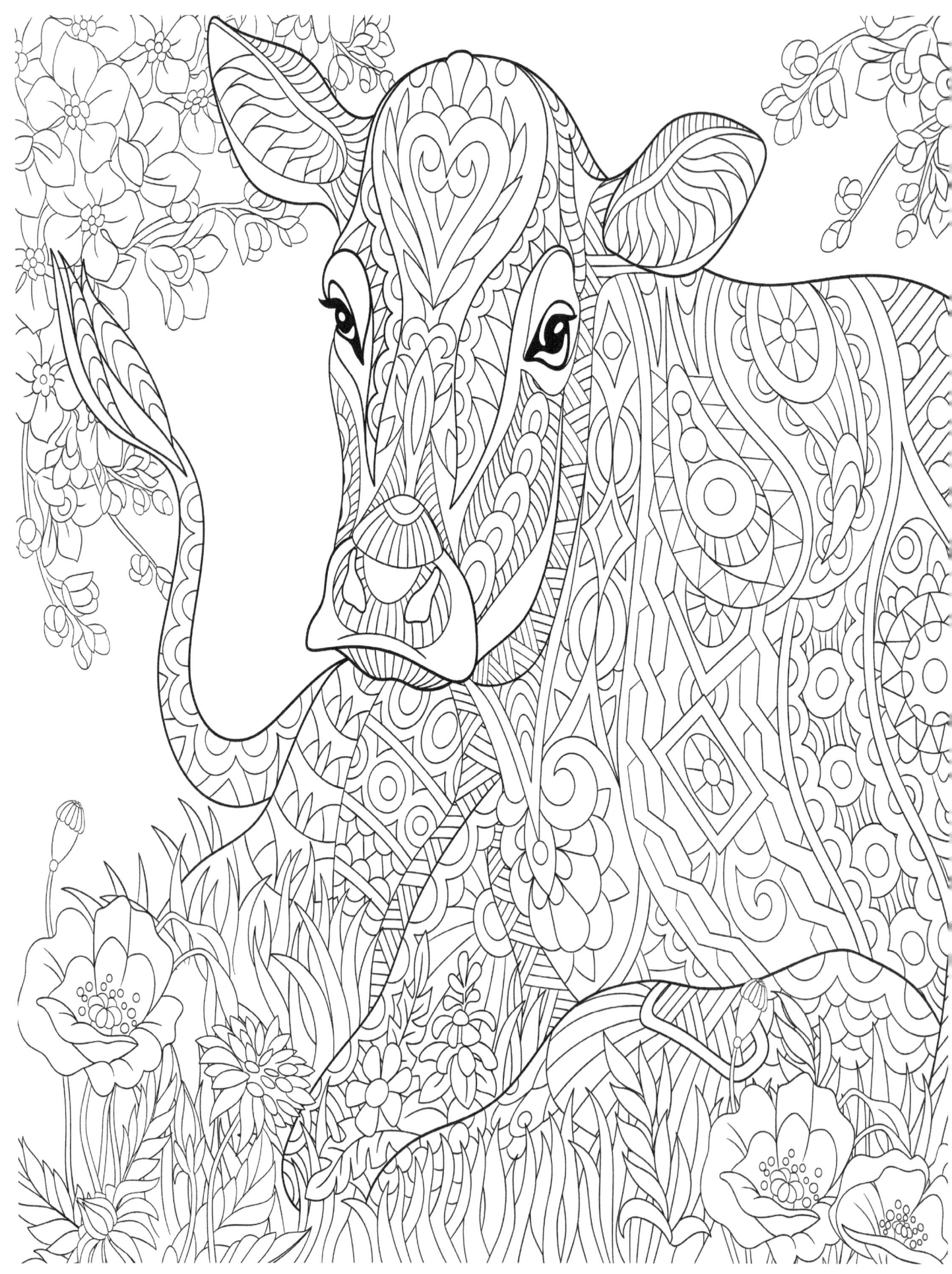

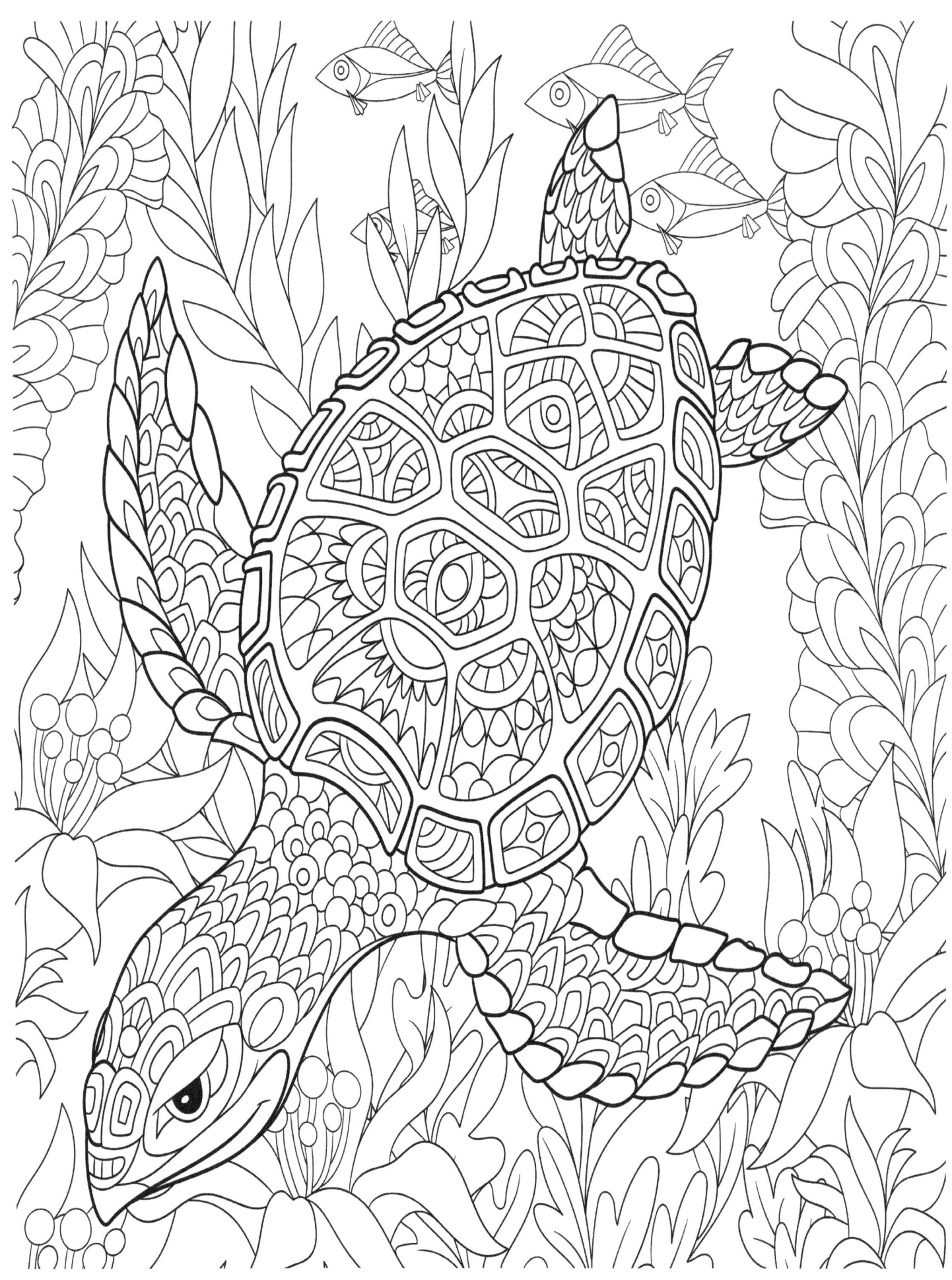

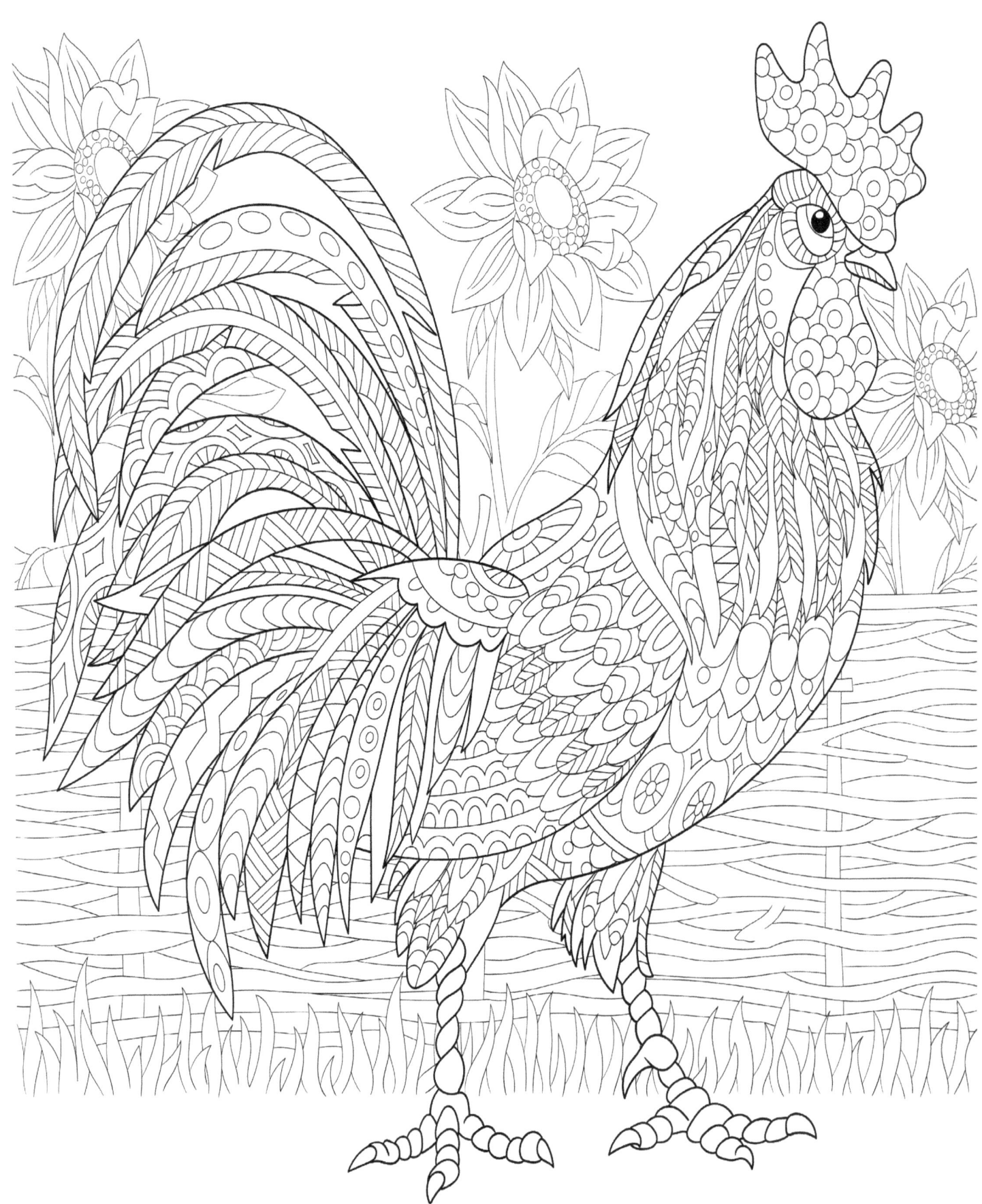

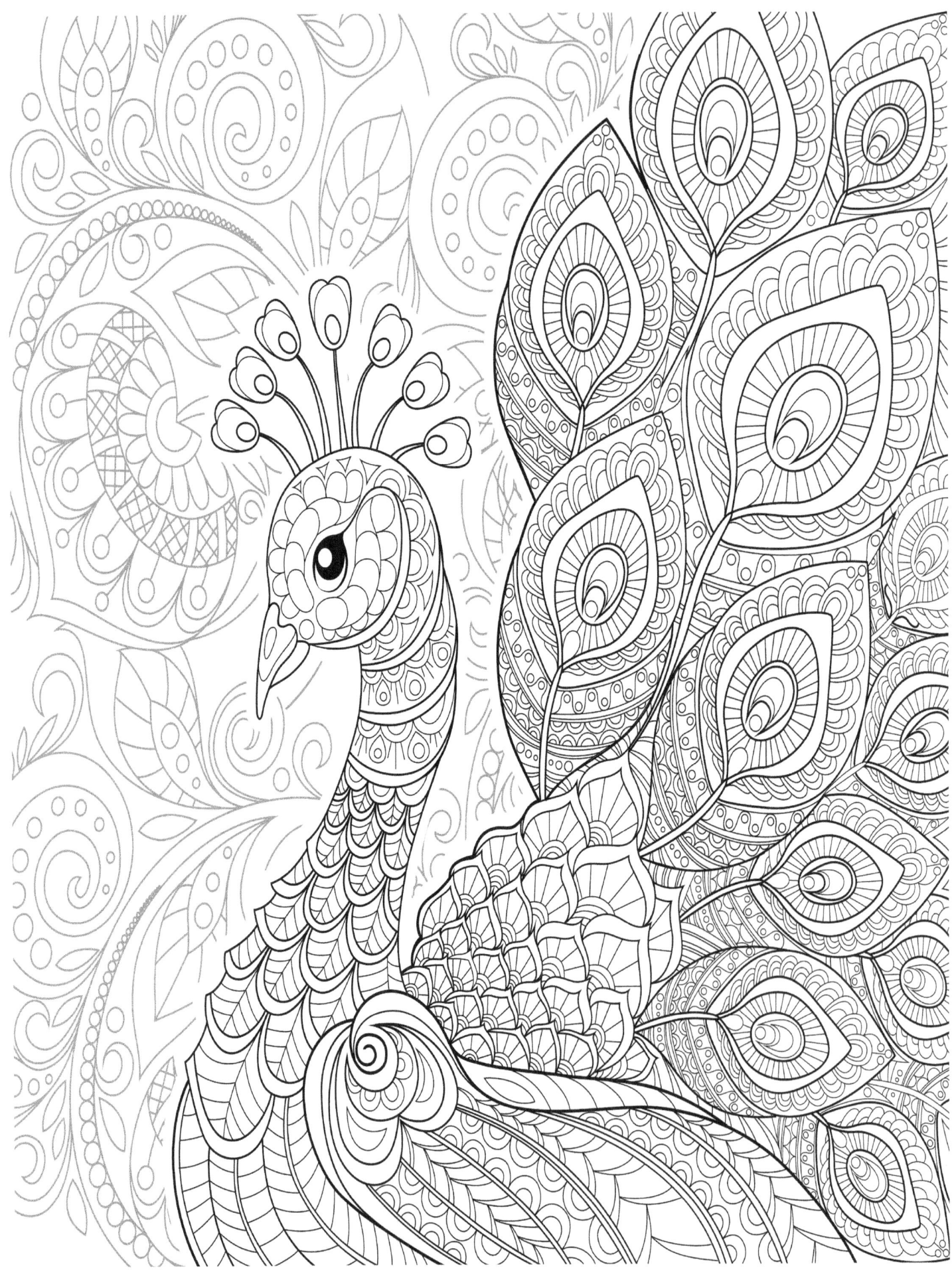

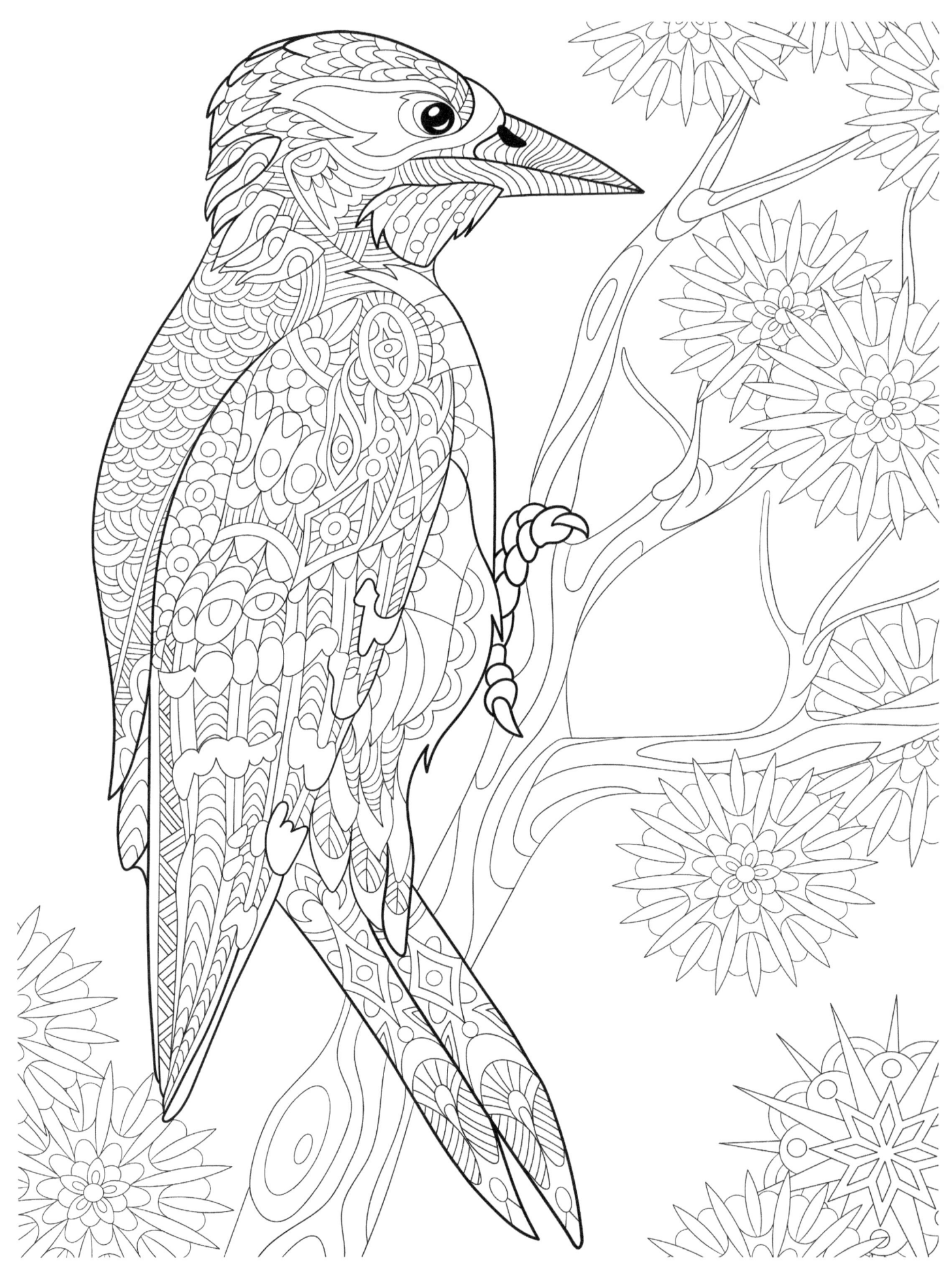

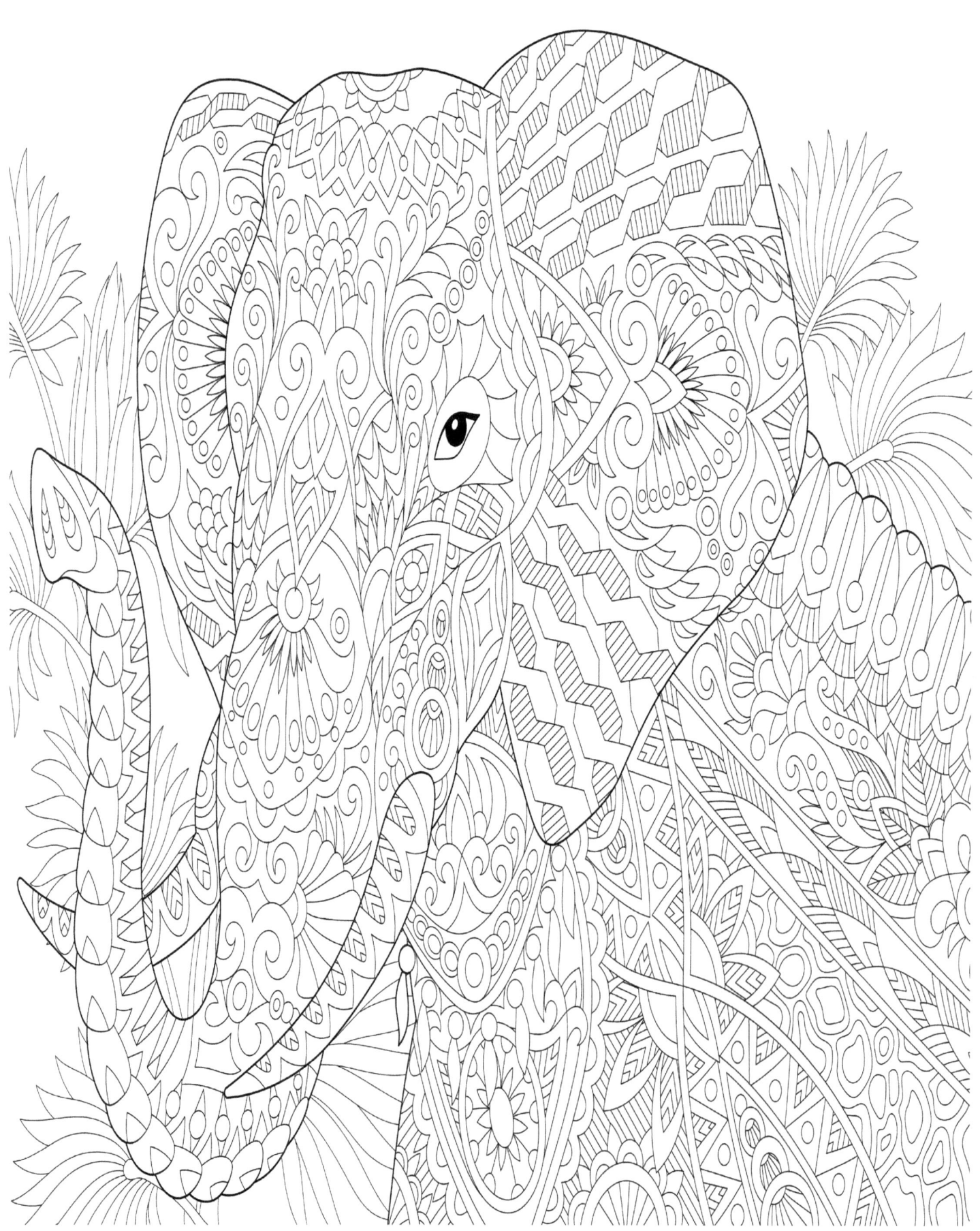

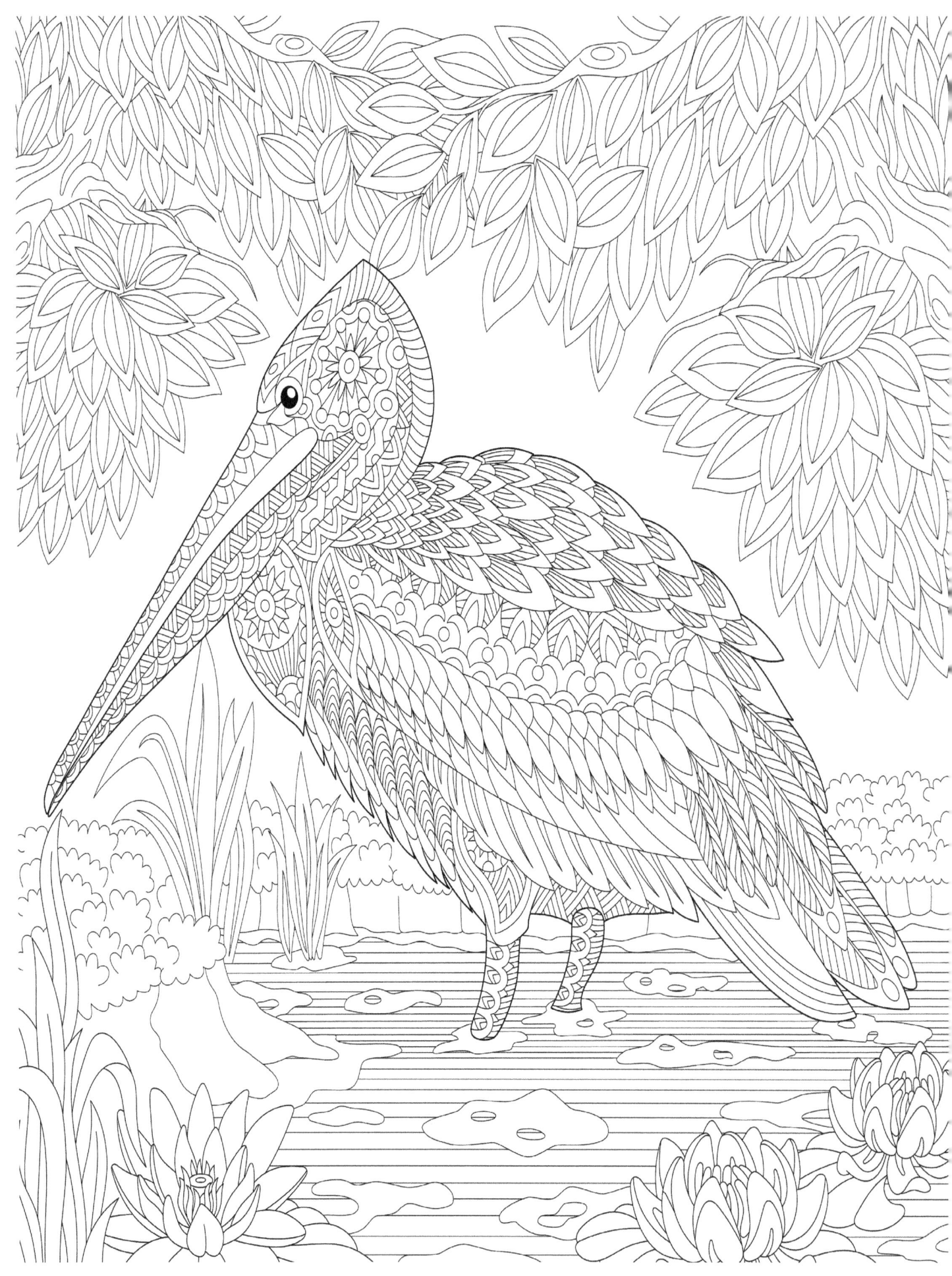

www.ingramcontent.com/pod-product-compliance
Lightning Source LLC
Chambersburg PA
CBHW082356220526
45470CB00008B/2770